D0970505

Presented to

Clear Lake City - County
Freeman Branch Library

By

Friends of the Freeman Library

Harris County
Public Library
your pathway to knowledge

IT'S OKAY TO MANAGE YOUR BOSS

THE STEP-BY-STEP PROGRAM FOR MAKING THE BEST OF YOUR MOST IMPORTANT RELATIONSHIP AT WORK

Bruce Tulgan

JOSSEY-BASS
A Wiley Imprint
www.josseybass.com

Published by Jossey-Bass
A Wiley Imprint
989 Market Street, San Francisco, CA 94103-1741—www.josseybass.com

Readers should be aware that Internet Web sites offered as citations and/or sources
for further information may have changed or disappeared between the time this was
written and when it is read.

Limit of Liability/Disclaimer of Warranty: While the publisher and author have
used their best efforts in preparing this book, they make no representations or
warranties with respect to the accuracy or completeness of the contents of this book
and specifically disclaim any implied warranties of merchantability or fitness for a
particular purpose. No warranty may be created or extended by sales representatives
or written sales materials. The advice and strategies contained herein may not be
suitable for your situation. You should consult with a professional where appropriate.
Neither the publisher nor author shall be liable for any loss of profit or any other
commercial damages, including but not limited to special, incidental, consequential,
or other damages.

Jossey-Bass books and products are available through most bookstores.
To contact Jossey-Bass directly call our Customer Care Department within the
U.S. at 800-956-7739, outside the U.S. at 317-572-3986, or fax 317-572-4002.

Jossey-Bass also publishes its books in a variety of electronic formats. Some content
that appears in print may not be available in electronic books.

Library of Congress Cataloging-in-Publication Data

Tulgan, Bruce.
  Its okay to manage your boss : the step-by-step program for making the best of your
most important relationship at work / Bruce Tulgan.
    p. cm.
  Includes index.
  ISBN 978-0-470-60530-1 (cloth); ISBN 978-0-470-90154-0 (ebk);
  978-0-470-90155-7 (ebk); 978-0-470-90156-4 (ebk)
  1. Managing your boss. I. Title.
  HF5548.83.T85 2010
  650.1'3—dc22

                                                              2010025177

Printed in the United States of America
FIRST EDITION
HB Printing   10 9 8 7 6 5 4 3 2 1

This book is dedicated to my parents,
Henry Tulgan & Norma Propp Tulgan

CONTENTS

CHAPTER ONE

Refuse to Be Undermanaged

You show up at work one day, and much of your job seems to be coming unglued: you have a voice mail from your manager telling you the project you worked so hard on for the last two weeks is all wrong. You think, *Well, I told you I didn't have enough experience to take that task on!* Then you receive an e-mail from a manager in another department who is hounding you about "taking way too long" with yet another project; you need to get that to her "immediately."

Meanwhile, you were planning to spend the morning finishing up one of your routine tasks—dotting some *i*'s and crossing a few *t*'s—but you've received so many urgent e-mails, you figure you better answer them before you do anything else. Last week the same scenario played out, and you forgot to go back and dot the *i*'s and cross the *t*'s; in the end, the task had to be redone at the last minute. You ended up working very late that day, and everybody was mad. You don't want to do that again, so you've been trying to lie low and stay out of everybody's way. But now you have these managers messing with your day before it even starts!

What's going on? You think of yourself as a high-performer. But you start second-guessing yourself: *One manager tells me to do one thing. Another tells me to do something totally different. How am I supposed to know what takes priority? How am I supposed to know what is up to me and what's not? The bosses here don't have any idea how to manage! Only rarely does one of them spend enough time with me to give me the guidance I need, or to make sure I have the resources to do the job, or to help me problem-solve. Half the time I don't get any recognition for the work I do well, no matter how hard I work.*

If this is anything like your situation at work, either now or sometime in the recent past, then you are not alone!

What's going on here?

It is tempting to look at the scenario described above and blame the managers or even the entire enterprise. Maybe this company has a disproportionate number of managers who are true jerks—but probably not. It is more likely that the problem is hiding in plain sight: *Undermanagement.*

Across all industries and at all levels of organizations there is a shocking and profound epidemic of what I call undermanagement. It is the opposite of micromanagement. The vast majority of supervisory relationships between employees and their bosses lack the day-to-day engagement necessary to consistently maintain the very basics of management: clear expectations; necessary resources; real performance tracking; and fair credit and reward. In fact, most employees report that they feel disengaged from their immediate boss(es); that two-way communication is sorely deficient; and that employees rarely get the daily guidance, resources, feedback, and reward that they need.

In my book *It's Okay to Be the Boss*, I explored the causes of our pernicious undermanagement epidemic and tried to show readers how just about any problem in any workplace can be traced back to a case of undermanagement. Although *undermanagement* is not a household word like *micromanagement*, it should be, because undermanagement is a success-crushing syndrome, and it is worth fighting against. Indeed, the following consequences of undermanagement make the impact of micromanagement look like nothing:

- Unnecessary problems arise.
- Small problems, which could have been solved easily, turn into big problems.
- Resources are squandered.
- Employees perform tasks and carry out responsibilities the wrong way for longer periods of time.
- Low-performers hang around, causing problems for everyone else (and collecting the same paycheck as everyone else, too!).
- High-performers get frustrated, lose commitment, and think about leaving.
- Employees are not set up to perform at their best.
- Managers spend their management time in all the wrong ways.

You may not be aware of undermanagement in your workplace. But look around you. I bet undermanagement is costing *you* every single day. It robs you of positive experiences in the workplace and prevents you from reaching greater success. Undermanagement gets in the way of your learning and development, makes it harder for you to optimize relationships, and diminishes your opportunities for new tasks, responsibilities, and projects. Undermanagement very likely causes you to earn less than you should and prevents you from gaining more flexibility in your schedule and in other work conditions.

So who is responsible for this undermanagement epidemic? After all, isn't it the manager's job to manage? Shouldn't the bosses be taking charge? Yes. And I believe managing is a sacred responsibility. If there's a problem, the boss is the solution. If you are the boss, then you are the one everyone is counting on.

Unfortunately, too many leaders, managers, and supervisors are failing to lead, manage, and supervise. They simply do not take charge on a day-to-day basis. They fail to spell out expectations every step of the way, ensure that necessary resources are in place, track performance, correct failure, and reward success. They don't know how to, they don't want to, or they are just afraid to.

Most managers are under a tremendous amount of pressure. They typically move into supervisory positions because they are very good at something, but not usually because they are especially good at managing people. Once promoted, most new managers receive very little in the way of effective management training. And the legacy of leadership in most organizations great and small is still "hands off": "Here's the mission. Figure it out. Wait for us to notice you. We'll let you know if you do something wrong, and the system will reward you the same as everyone else."

The pendulum of management thinking, books, and training has also swung in the exactly same, wrong direction toward hands-off management. Popular books have naively insisted that employees do their best work when they are free to manage themselves. According to this false-empowerment approach, employees should "own" their work and be free to make their own decisions. Managers are merely facilitators; they should not tell employees how to do their jobs but rather let them come up with their own methods. Make employees feel good inside, and results will take care of themselves.

But let's face it. You know very well that somebody is in charge and that you will be held accountable. You do not have the power to do things your own way; you are not free to ignore tasks you don't like; you are not free to do as you please. You can only make your own decisions within defined guidelines and parameters that are determined by others according to the strict logic of the enterprise at hand.

When your managers give you responsibility without sufficient direction and support, that is not empowering you. That is downright negligence. Unfortunately, most managers have bought this false-empowerment philosophy and don't take a stronger hand when it comes to managing; they don't even perform the basic tasks of managing. Most managers, then, undermanage. Here are the top seven reasons why they undermanage and how that affects you directly:

One: They are afraid of micromanaging

I often say that micromanagement is a giant red herring. Is there even such a thing as "micromanagement" at all? Of course, some managers overdo it sometimes, but the vast majority *underdo* it. Real micromanagement, if it exists at all, is quite rare. The funny thing is that most cases mistaken for micromanagement turn out to be undermanagement in disguise. Let me show this through three scenarios:

1. Your manager asks you to check in with him every step of the way in order to make basic decisions or take simple actions. Is this a case of micromanagement? No. If an employee is unable to make basic decisions or take simple actions on his own, it's almost always because the manager has not prepared the employee in advance to do so. Your manager must make sure you understand how to accomplish your tasks and carry out your responsibilities and must equip you with the tools and skills you need to do your job.

2. You make decisions and take actions without ever checking in with your manager. When she finds out about them, you get in big trouble. Burned for taking initiative? Yes. Micromanagement? No. If an employee does not know where her discretion begins and ends, that's because the manager has not spelled out guidelines and parameters for the employee up front. Your manager has to painstakingly clarify what is within your authority to do, and what is not.

3. Your manager is constantly tangled up in your tasks, or you are getting tangled up in your manager's tasks—in the end, you just can't tell which tasks belong to the manager and which ones belong to you. Isn't that micromanagement? No. It is a result of your manager's failure to delegate. Your manager has to spell out exactly which tasks belong to you and which ones belong to her.

Of course, there are cases in which managers do overdo it. Sometimes this is the result of an obsessive-compulsive manager or a manager who wants an assistant at his beck and call—and that is not a management relationship. Or maybe it's just the manager's first day managing a new employee. The good news is that when managers accidentally manage too closely, they can just step back a little. No harm done. But if they undermanage, the harm is pervasive and damaging to everyone involved.

Two: They are afraid of being unfair by not treating all employees the same

Where does this fear come from? First, an aversion to any kind of litigation risk has led to a blanket default presumption in the working world that differential treatment of employees is "against the rules." Second, political correctness has caused many people to self-censor any mention of differences between and among individuals—even observable merit-based differences. Third, a popular misunderstanding of psychology and human development theory has people mistakenly believing that in essence, "we are all winners." Thus, the underlying theory that many managers have walked away with is that because every person has innate value, we should treat everybody the same.

This sense of false fairness often means managers are unwilling to provide employees with extra rewards when they go the extra mile. Since managers can't do everything for everybody, most of them take the easy way out, rewarding nobody specially. Limited resources for rewards are further watered down by trying to spread them around equally. The result: low- and mediocre-performers enjoy the same rewards as high-performers such as yourself! When your manager suffers from this "false fairness" syndrome, she fails to give you—her best employee—the flexibility you need to continue working hard and smart, and deprives herself of a key tool for motivating her employees. What's truly fair is giving you the chance to earn more or less on the basis of your actual performance.

Three: They are afraid of being perceived as a "jerk" and want to be seen as "nice"

Surprisingly, what I call the "false nice-guy complex" is more widespread than you can imagine. False nice-guy managers refuse to make decisions, give orders, and hold people ac-countable. They tell themselves they are abdicating these re-sponsibilities because they don't want to be a "jerk." The irony is that false nice guys tend to soft-pedal their authority so much that things are bound to go wrong. When they do, these bosses get frustrated and angry, and tend to act like jerks: arbitrary, out of line, loud, mean, and even abusive. Afterwards, they feel terribly guilty for behaving this way. So what do they do? They go back to soft-pedaling their authority, without ever realizing that they are caught in a vicious cycle.

Are they really being nice-guy managers by failing to pro-vide the direction, support, and coaching that employees need in order to succeed? In truth, they are simply letting themselves off the hook to avoid the uncomfortable tension that comes with being stuck between the boardroom and the front lines—being the one who has to negotiate the competing needs and desires of the employer and the employee. They are refusing to take responsibility for their authority, which has real consequences that are anything but nice: problems arise, sometimes big ones. When problems are not dealt with, they may turn into disasters. The best way for a manager to avoid being a jerk is to accept his or her legitimate authority and feel comfortable using it. Genuine nice-guy managers do what it takes to help employees succeed so that those employees can deliver great service to customers and earn more rewards for themselves.

Yes, of course, some managers are true jerks. Here are the seven common true-jerk boss personas:

1. The boss who lets small problems slide over and over again, but then comes down like a ton of bricks when one of those problems gets out of control.
2. The boss who is compulsive or obsessive and imposes that on you.
3. The boss who doesn't want to manage but wants a beck-and-call assistant.
4. The boss who pretends things are up to you when they are not.
5. The boss who doesn't keep track of what's going on but makes big decisions that affect everyone.
6. The boss who soft-pedals his authority until something goes terribly wrong, and then comes in and chews you out.
7. The boss who is intimidating, mean, or abusive.

In Chapter Nine I will go into detail with each of these personas and provide best practices for dealing with these types of true-jerk boss.

Four: They are afraid of having difficult confrontations with employees

Lots of managers find that the most painful aspect of managing is having difficult conversations, even confrontations, with employees. Such managers often avoid day-to-day conversations with employees about their work because they are trying to avoid these confrontations. But when your manager avoids talking with you about your day-to-day work, then confrontations actually become more likely. Why?

If you and your boss are not having regular conversations about your work, then neither one of you is experienced at them. If you and your boss are not talking regularly, your boss has probably not been making expectations clear. When a problem absolutely must be dealt with and he finally confronts you, both of you are more likely to be frustrated and angry. The conversation will not only come as a big unpleasant surprise to you but is more likely to become heated. There is only one way managers can avoid difficult confrontations: having lots of mundane conversations about the day-to-day work before anything goes wrong!

Five: They are afraid to break organizational rules and procedures and feel constrained by bureaucratic red tape

Managers tell me every day that despite their best efforts, they are held back by bureaucratic rules, regulations, and red tape. Many find navigating organizational procedures and legal requirements daunting. Some, in fact, have gotten into real trouble for purposely or inadvertently doing something wrong. Still more have found themselves tangled up in endless paperwork, meetings, and calls regarding a personnel issue, often with a very unsatisfying end for everybody involved.

Dealing with all the complexities of employment rules and organizational procedures can be a pain in the neck. Still, some managers hide behind this challenge as an excuse to avoid managing. Others work through the challenge every day in order to make sure the employees they manage are getting the management basics. How should your manager work within and around the rules? She should learn them backward and forward—and then work them. Performance is always the fair and legal basis for discriminating in the workplace. As long as your boss can demonstrate that any rewards or detriments to you are based solely on your work performance, there is no basis for a claim of unlawful discrimination. Would you want it any other way?

Six: They are natural leaders, but not very good at managing

Yes, some of your managers might be gifted natural leaders. If so, then congratulations are due. The natural leader is, of course, blessed with a rare gift. And you are fortunate to have a gifted natural leader to follow. Fortunate, maybe. You see, lots of natural leaders are not such great managers. They might be visionary, charismatic, articulate, and unusually energetic. They might be motivating and inspirational, and people may want to follow them. But sometimes they rely too heavily on their natural gifts and don't pay enough attention to the management basics. As a result, they may build people up, but sometimes they build people up to fail.

Missing in most workplaces are leaders at all levels who consistently practice the basics of management: providing direction and guidance, holding people accountable, dealing with failure, and rewarding success. These are the most important practices when it comes to helping you get work done better and faster, avoid unnecessary problems, solve problems quickly, stay on track, succeed, and earn more of the credit and rewards you need and want. Managers don't need to be natural leaders to do this; all they need to do is consistently practice the basics of management.

Seven: They feel like they don't have enough time to spend managing you

Most managers get caught in a time trap: managers feel like they don't have enough time to manage, so they avoid having regular one-on-one conversations with employees to make sure they are on track. As a result, things go wrong, sometimes terribly wrong. When things go wrong, managers have no choice but to spend a bunch of time fixing problems that never should have happened in the first place. By the time managers are done fixing whatever has gone wrong, they *really* feel like they don't have enough time to manage.

Good managers know that they can't afford *not* to spend time managing you. They have regular one-on-one conversations with their employees, setting expectations, goals, and deadlines; assigning necessary resources; solving problems; correcting course; reviewing work in progress; and planning next steps. If your boss does that with you for a few weeks, then mark my words: more and more of your conversations will be "good news" conversations; there will be few problems to fix; and your boss won't be wasting any time.

WHEN THEY UNDERMANAGE, YOU PAY THE PRICE

Whatever is behind your bosses' undermanagement tendencies and despite the lack of management support you receive, *you* are still expected to meet today's higher expectations on the job. *You* are under more pressure. *You* are expected to work longer, harder, smarter, faster, and better. There's no room for downtime, waste, or inefficiency. *You* must learn and use new technologies, processes, and skills, all the while adjusting to ongoing organizational changes. *You* receive less guidance and support, work in smaller teams with greater requirements, and have less time to rest, recuperate, and prepare. And *you* want to know, "Boss, what do you want from me?"

Perhaps getting answers to this question has always been hard, but in the workplace of the not-so-distant past, at least you could count on job security and long-term vesting rewards. As long as you kept your head down and your mouth shut and did as you were told, you had a good shot at staying employed and climbing the ladder. There was a good chance you would work for the same boss for a long time. Maybe you would both climb the ladder together in the organization. In the workplace of the past, nobody held your hand either, but in return you could hope that the system would take care of you in the long run.

Not anymore.

Nowadays, the world is highly interconnected, fiercely competitive, knowledge-driven, and global. Employers are geared for constant change. In order to survive, they need to get more and better work out of fewer people, squeeze cost out of the process, and be lean and flexible. That means you need to be increasingly aggressive in order to take care of yourself and your family. Why would you trust the "system" or the organization to take care of you over time?

The chain of command is also no longer clear in most organizations. Most organizations have become flatter as layers of management have been removed in the last decade. More employees are being managed by short-term project leaders instead of "organization-chart managers." Who has authority over employees? The answer often depends on the project, task, and responsibility. Who is in charge? Whoever has control of resources, work conditions, and rewards. To whom do *you* answer today? If you are like most employees, you answer to multiple bosses—some directly, others indirectly. You are often pulled in different directions by these authority figures who have competing interests and agendas. All of them have the ability to improve or worsen your daily work conditions, your chances of getting rewards, and your long-term career prospects. And all of them are different. Some are great. Some are good. Some are mediocre. Some are pretty bad. And some are downright horrible. Then, too, some are true jerks. They each have their own style, strengths, and weaknesses.

Under these circumstances, *you* are the only one *you* can control. You can control your role and conduct in each of these relationships. You can control how you manage these relationships and how you get what you need from them. And you have no choice: if you want to survive, succeed, and prosper, *you* have to get really good at managing your bosses.

Why?

The boss—at every level—is the most important person in the workplace today. On this there is widespread consensus. Study after study shows that the relationship employees have with their bosses is the number one factor in the ability of employees to produce high-quality work consistently, to feel good about work, and to earn credit, flexible work conditions, and greater rewards.

You rely on your immediate boss more than on any other individual for meeting your basic needs and expectations at work, and for dealing with just about any issue that arises at work. The boss is your point of contact. But much more than that, on a daily basis the boss defines your work experience. To become and remain a consistent high-performer, you need bosses who are strong and highly engaged, who know exactly who you are and exactly what you are doing every step of the way. You need bosses who let you know that you are important and that your work is important. You need bosses who spell out expectations clearly; who teach you best practices; who warn you of pitfalls; who help you solve small problems before they fester and grow; and who reward you when you go the extra mile. You want bosses who will set you up for success and thereby help you earn what you need and want from the job, every step of the way.

Your ability to manage these relationships will have the single greatest impact on your productivity, performance, morale, and ability to earn credit and rewards for your contributions. You need strong bosses, and you are going to have to help them get there. That means you need to take charge and start managing your boss. You need to take responsibility for your role and your conduct in every single management relationship with every single boss.

For a lot of people the idea of taking responsibility for managing their boss requires a fundamental rethinking of their role and their relationships in the workplace. The thought of "managing your boss" is a challenging one. The boss is above you, over you, and in charge of you—the employee. Even if you are a manager yourself, when you are dealing with your boss, you are the employee.

But because your boss is the key to getting what you need to survive and succeed at work, you need a strategy for managing your boss and practical tactics that work in a world of constantly shifting, complex authority relationships.

BAD ADVICE FOR MANAGING YOUR BOSS

Developing a strategy for managing your boss and dealing with the highly complex authority relationships in your workplace is tougher than it appears. Not only is the advice doled out by experts not always helpful, but most of us are so used to being undermanaged that most of us have bought into a myth of how we ought to be managed by our bosses or how we ought to behave at work.

If you are looking for guidance on how to manage your boss, zillions of so-called experts out there will be happy to provide it. The problem is that so much of the advice about "managing up" or "managing your boss" doesn't tell the whole story.

Some experts offer advice only for dealing with an incompetent boss or a bully, but they fail to see that unless you've been managing your boss closely, you won't even know if you are dealing with an incompetent or a bully.

Other experts suggest that you cater to your boss and follow him or her up the ladder, but this approach is stuck in the outmoded view that supervisory relationships are simple, fixed, long term, and hierarchical. Most supervisory relationships today are complex, shifting, short term, and transactional, so you have to be prepared to adapt to the many bosses you are likely to have over time, and pursue your own career.

Other experts advocate manipulating your boss to meet your personal needs. But playing your boss to squeeze out as much benefit for you as you possibly can in exchange for the least effort on your part is self-serving, deceptive, and dishonorable. When you constantly take advantage of your boss, you are in a dead-end relationship.

Finally, some experts argue you should "partner" with your boss, but they fail to acknowledge the importance of the power differential in a boss-employee relationship. Your boss is your boss precisely because he or she has authority, influence, and control of resources that directly affect you.

Dovetailing with all of this so-called expert advice are many widespread misconceptions about how we ought to relate to our bosses. I ask people in the workplace every day why they don't take a stronger hand when it comes to managing their bosses. They almost always give me the same reasons. The most common myths, explained below, discourage so many employees at all levels from taking more responsibility for their relationships with managers.

Myth 1: If you are a high-performer, then your boss shouldn't tell you how to do your job

No matter how good you may be at your job, everybody needs guidance, direction, and support in order to succeed. You don't want to waste your valuable time and energy doing the wrong things or doing the right things the wrong way. Right? Even if you know more about the specific task, responsibility, or project than your boss does, you are not operating in a vacuum.

You need to make sure your work fits with your company's overall mission. You need to have goals articulated and the guidelines and parameters for your tasks and responsibilities spelled out. You need to be given concrete deadlines, clear timelines, and reasonable performance benchmarks to meet. And your boss is the person who needs to communicate these requirements to you and to make sure you stay on track. That's the only way to become and remain a high-performer. (But if you are a high-performer, you probably already know all that.)

Myth 2: In order to be creative at work, you need to be left alone to do things your own way

If you really want to be creative at work, the first thing you need to know is exactly what is up to you, and what is not. So much of what gets done at work is simply not up to you. You need to know the requirements of every task, responsibility, or project before you can even think about being creative. Even if you are in a creative position, only when you know what is actually up to you will you have uncovered the small space in which you can be creative.

Myth 3: If someone else is getting special treatment, then you should too

If someone else is getting special treatment, then figure out exactly what that person did to earn the special treatment and what exactly you need to do to earn the special treatment you want for yourself. How would it be fair to treat everybody in a workplace exactly the same? That's only fair if you are running a commune. The reality is that we are not all winners, as everybody knows. Treating everybody the same, regardless of their performance, is totally unfair. If your coworkers are receiving rewards that you are not getting, take that as a big reality check. What you need is a fair and accurate assessment of your performance so that you can continually improve, and thereby earn more of the rewards you want.

Don't be the squeaky wheel asking for more. Be the self-starting high-performer who is constantly *earning* more.

Myth 4: The path to success is catering to your boss's style and preferences

Your boss's style and preferences may or may not be smart business practices. Your best path to success is making sure you get clear and realistic expectations every step of the way, the necessary resources to complete your tasks, fair and accurate and honest feedback, and appropriate recognition and rewards for your work.

It is true that you need to align yourself as best you can with what works for each of your bosses. Some bosses prefer updates in writing; others prefer verbal reports. Some bosses prefer big-picture reports. Others like to keep track of the details. You should certainly try to tune in to each boss's preferences, but you cannot afford to compromise the basic elements you need in order to succeed. If your boss prefers that you "take a stab" at a project without giving you clear expectations, then you had better probe a little: "Exactly how long do you want me to dedicate to 'taking a stab'? Are there any things that

I absolutely may not, should not, can not do while 'taking a stab'?" If your boss is not forthcoming with feedback, you need to find a way to monitor, measure, and document your own performance. If your boss's style doesn't include giving fair credit and rewards for great performance, then how much longer are you going to be giving your great performance to that manager?

Myth 5: "Making friends" with your boss is smart workplace politics

False friendships are a waste of time. Real friendships may be wonderful in your personal life, but they are likely to complicate your situation at work. The smartest workplace politics is to keep your work relationships focused on the work. That is not to say that real friendships do not or should not occur in the workplace. Of course they do. Real friendships develop over time at work, including friendships with people who are your boss. If that's your situation, then you'll have to work hard to protect that friendship from the realities of the workplace. That means you need to manage your boss very well, not just for the sake of your success at work but also for the sake of your friendship.

In the vast majority of situations, however, your boss is not actually a friend. Maybe you two shoot the breeze. Maybe once in a while you have a brief personal connection, a moment of sharing something personal. You interact at the occasional formal or informal social event outside of work. The problem is that this sort of rapport is very thin, and it collapses the moment the work gets serious.

What is the best workplace politics? Build authentic relationships with your bosses by developing genuine rapport, regardless of whether you are friends. How? By talking about the work on a regular basis. This is what the two of you have in common that is authentic. This is the kind of rapport that makes the work go better, that won't collapse as soon as the work gets serious.

Myth 6: Hiding from mistakes and problems is a good way to avoid trouble

The best way to avoid trouble is to immediately come clean about the details of any mistakes or problems as they occur, as part of your regular, one-on-one dialogues with your boss about the work. When you deal with mistakes and problems as they occur, you are much more likely to solve them while they are still small and manageable, before they have gotten out of control.

When you gloss over small mistakes without solving them, they sometimes drift away—but they are more likely to recur. Those recurring small problems may become part of the fabric of your work, but sometimes small problems that recur incessantly cause difficult confrontations, as when coworkers or the boss finally explode in an outburst of frustration.

Even more serious, small mistakes and problems may fester and grow and, over time, become big problems. By the time you have a conversation with your boss about the problem, it's usually too late. Why is this? First, solving a problem after it has festered is much more difficult than preventing that problem in the first place, or solving it while it was smaller. Much time and energy has to be spent cleaning up the mess. Second, in the midst of a problem, neither you nor the boss in question is going to be at your best. By then everybody is stressed, frustrated, and in a hurry. Sometimes these conversations become heated. Your boss is likely to feel that she has spent her management time "fighting fires," thus getting behind on her "real" work. Sometimes it's hard to start feeling good about working with this boss again after a difficult confrontation.

No problem is so small that it should be left alone. If you include regular problem solving in your ongoing one-on-one dialogues with every single boss, then nine out of ten performance problems will be solved quickly and easily, or altogether avoided. Helping your boss nitpick at the small mistakes and problems in your work is a good thing. It sends a message to your boss that high performance is your focus and that you realize that details matter.

Myth 7: No news is good news, but being "coached" on your performance is bad news

No news may not be bad, but it definitely does you no good. Being coached on your performance, on the other hand, is an opportunity to improve—and that is always good news.

Why does "performance coaching" have a bad name among so many in the workplace? One reason is surely that most bosses think of coaching an employee only when they think the employee has a recurring performance problem, such as missed deadlines, poor work quality, or a bad attitude toward customers or coworkers.

But why should performance coaching only be about addressing performance problems? The voice of performance coaching is steady and persistent, relentlessly methodical, hands-on, enthusiastic, and pushy. It is the constant banter of focus, improvement, and accountability: "What can I teach you right now? What can you improve right now?" A great coach helps you remember to be purposeful about every detail to build your skills. From focusing, you learn focus itself.

Obviously, some bosses have more natural talent than others when it comes to coaching. Keep your eyes peeled and your ears open for opportunities to be coached by your bosses, or by anyone who is an objective, encouraging voice with experience and wisdom to share. Don't listen for those hollering, "Rah! Rah!" around your workplace. Don't be fooled by contrived enthusiasm. Look for the real teachers among your bosses, and soak up their teachings. Assure the boss that you very much welcome candid feedback in detail, both positive and corrective. Try to turn every conversation with your boss into a coaching session.

Myth 8: If your boss doesn't like to read paperwork, you don't need to keep track of your performance in writing

You owe it to yourself and the organization to keep track of everything you do in writing. Most managers monitor employee performance only incidentally, as when they happen to observe the employee working; when they are presented with the employee's work product; when there is a big win; or when there is a notable problem. They rarely document employee performance unless they are required to do so, leaving no written track record other than those bottom-line reports that tell so little about the day-to-day actions of an employee. Whether or not your boss keeps track of your day-to-day performance in writing, *you* should. Here are six reasons why:

Reason 1: You probably have a lot to keep track of at work and need a tracking system to document it all.

Reason 2: Keeping track your performance in writing will help you add clarity to your working relationship with each boss. Writing down the details of your one-on-one conversations with your boss is a good way to avoid misunderstandings over what was said about what, and when. If you get in the habit, together with each boss, of tracking your conversations in writing, then you are more likely to stay on the same page.

Reason 3: Tracking your own performance in writing will help you and your boss create a shared commitment to the expectations you agree on and document together.

Reason 4: Written tracking is the key to your ongoing performance improvement. Constant evaluation and feedback help you revise and adjust your performance, and they help your boss revise and adjust her marching orders to you. In order to do that, you have to keep score—in writing.

Reason 5: When you document your performance in writing on an ongoing basis, you will be in a stronger position to make the case for receiving more generous rewards or applying for promotions based on your valuable contributions.

Reason 6: If you document your performance on a continuing basis, you will help your boss complete the review process in ways that reflect more accurately your actual day-to-day performance.

Myth 9: If you are not a "people person," then you'll have a hard time getting ahead in the workplace

Some people are unusually charismatic, observant, receptive, quick-witted, articulate, engaging, energetic, and likeable. No doubt, these Princes and Princesses Charming have a big advantage over the rest of us. But charm alone doesn't cut it in today's fiercely competitive, rapidly changing, knowledge-driven, global, and nonstop world. The key to getting ahead in today's workplace and the wider free market for talent is being really good at consistently delivering valuable contributions at a swift, steady pace, while constantly adapting to changing circumstances. That takes more than relationship mojo.

If you happen to be one of these natural "people persons," then you are very blessed. But I'm afraid that won't be enough in today's world. To succeed, you also have to consistently practice the basics of self-management and boss management. If you take personal responsibility for your role and your conduct in your working relationship with your bosses and make sure you are managing every boss closely every step of the way, you'll be worth your weight in gold—even if you don't call people by name, look people in the eye when you talk, smile, or "back-channel" in conversations.

Whether or not you are a people person, learn proven techniques for self-management and boss management, and practice those techniques diligently until they become skills, and then habits. Don't try to be someone you are not. Be yourself. Be genuine. Relax. Then follow the proven techniques and practice, practice, practice.

Myth 10: Some bosses are just too busy to meet with you

No matter how busy your boss may be, your boss does not have time *not* to meet with you on a regular basis.

Don't get me wrong. You should be very careful about wasting even one minute of your bosses' time—or anybody's time, for that matter. Your bosses have their own tasks, responsibilities, and projects besides their management obligations to you and their other direct-reports. Your boss is busy. You are busy. Nobody has a minute to waste.

That's exactly why neither you nor your boss has time to *not* meet regularly to talk about your work. When your boss doesn't spend time with you one-on-one, expectations often remain unclear; misunderstandings occur; you don't get the resources you need; you don't receive regular feedback to guide you; and even if you succeed against all odds, you probably won't get the credit you deserve.

But how often can you succeed against all odds? Without clear expectations, adequate resources, monitoring, and measuring of performance, the boss who tried so hard to avoid spending time managing you ends up spending lots of time managing you anyway—only now you are set up to fail instead of being set up to succeed. That's because small problems pile up or fester unattended until they become so big that they cannot be ignored. At that point, the boss has no choice but to chase them down and solve them, and then feel even more pressed for time. As a result, he goes right back to avoiding spending time managing you; so, the next occasion that he'll make time for management is when there is another big problem to chase down and solve.

Make your one-on-one time with every boss brief, straightforward, efficient, and all about the work. But make sure you get that regular time with every boss you answer to directly. If you push your bosses to put the management time where it belongs—up front, before anything goes right, wrong, or average—you will be sure to get the basic elements you need to succeed. If you make sure that the time every boss spends with you is effective and that it pays off in productivity, bosses are going to want to give you that time. You will gain a reputation for making good use of management time.

GETTING PAST THE MYTHS

All managers would prefer to manage self-starting high-performers who do tons of work very well and very fast without any guidance or support, who make no mistakes, and who have very few needs and expectations. I promise you, if given their druthers, just about all managers would opt for this type of employee. The only problem is that this type of employee doesn't exist. Only the very worst managers actually manage as if this fantasyland could possibly be true. They want you to do everything on your own. But when you do everything on your own, you are not likely to have anywhere near as much success as you would with the guidance, support, and engagement of a boss who is experienced, knowledgeable, and effective.

You have only two choices when working with such managers. You can avoid them and hope they find another employee to entangle and ignore. Or whenever possible you can manage that boss so closely that she either learns to engage with you effectively or else decides she would rather deal with someone who will be content to operate blindly in a sink-or-swim environment. Good riddance.

Great managers, by contrast, don't just want to work with high-flying superstar employees. And while they don't want to work either with lazy low-performers who don't care about the work and are not motivated to succeed, they are happy to work with employees at all levels of ability, skill, and experience. Great managers are ready to help you learn and grow. But if you want to get a lot of attention from the truly great managers, know this: great managers will expect you to take responsibility for your role and your conduct in the management relationship. If you want them to manage you, you had better be prepared to manage them.

Even if you have a great boss, great bosses have bad days, bad weeks, and even bad months when they drop the ball in attending to their management responsibilities. Even great bosses make mistakes that will have a huge impact on you if you are not sharing responsibility in the management relationship.

Of course, you cannot always work for a great boss. All bosses have strengths and weaknesses when it comes to managing you. And in truth the vast majority of managers fall somewhere between the worst and the great. They wish employees would manage themselves, but they realize that's not possible. They are stuck in some bad habits, but they can be drawn into better management habits. With these managers, you will earn dividends in exact proportion to the effort you put in.

GETTING THE MOST OUT OF YOUR RELATIONSHIP WITH YOUR BOSS

Low-performers are usually looking for a boss who is hands-off and treats every employee the same. They want a boss who doesn't know who is doing what where, why, when, or how—a boss who doesn't keep track and ignores performance problems. Low-performers want a boss who doesn't tell them what to do and how to do it, who doesn't spell out expectations every step of the way, who leaves them alone to hide and then collect the same paycheck as everyone else, regardless of their performance. Low-performers are the great beneficiaries of undermanagement. If that's you, then this is not a book you are going to like.

This book is written for people who want to be high-performers. In order to be a high-performer in today's workplace, you need to create highly engaged relationships with every boss, whether that boss is great, awful, or somewhere in between.

No matter who your boss may be on any given day, no matter what his or her style and preferences may be, there are four basics that you absolutely must take responsibility for getting from that boss:

1. Clearly spelled-out and reasonable expectations, including specific guidelines and a concrete timetable.

2. The skills, tools, and resources necessary to meet those expectations, or else an acknowledgment that you are being asked to meet expectations without them.

3. Accurate and honest feedback about your performance as well as course-correcting direction when necessary.

4. The fair quid pro quo—recognition and rewards—in exchange for your performance.

I know it's a huge shift for most people—and probably for you—to be highly engaged in an ongoing dialogue about your work with every single boss. Indeed, many participants in my It's Okay to Manage Your Boss seminars tell me, "Nobody has ever said this to me. You are giving me permission to help my manager manage me. You are giving me permission to get the support I need from my managers." Many participants tell me this is common sense: "Of course it's my responsibility to make sure I am working closely with any manager. Management relationships are two-way relationships." But half of the participants in my seminars say just the opposite (at the beginning, anyway): "You must be crazy. This contradicts most everything

I've ever read about 'managing up' and been taught in classes about how to advance my career."

And they are right. Very few people are saying what I am saying. Managing bosses in the real world is very, very difficult, and there are no easy solutions.

When I start talking about these hard realities in my training seminars, participants start listening carefully. When I tell them that I don't have any easy answers because easy answers work only in fantasyland, they start nodding. Then I promise them that I do have lots of very hard solutions that will take lots of guts, skill, time, and discipline to implement. All I do in my seminars is teach frustrated individuals to copy what the most effective boss-managers are actually doing every day. I've broken down my approach to real-world boss-managing into seven concrete steps. I refer to them as the seven steps back to the basics of managing your boss:

Step 1: The first person you have to manage every day is yourself.

Step 2: Get in the habit of managing your boss every day.

Step 3: Take it one boss at a time, one day at a time.

Step 4: Make sure you understand what is expected of you.

Step 5: Assess and plan for the resources you need.

Step 6: Track your performance in writing every step of the way.

Step 7: To earn greater credit and rewards, go the extra mile.

I've trained thousands of employees in the art of applying these steps to build and maintain strong, highly engaged working relationships with their managers. If you follow these seven steps consistently and you still can't get what you need from your boss, then maybe your boss is truly a "jerk boss." I encourage you to read Chapter Nine of this book for advice on how to deal with that boss. But if you follow these steps every day, the more likely scenario is that you will succeed. I hear just about every day from people I've trained, and the word from the front line is that as a result of following these steps and working closer with their bosses, they are getting more work done better and faster, running into fewer problems, solving problems more quickly, wasting fewer resources, achieving greater success, and earning more credit and rewards for their effort.

Be the employee who says to every boss: "Great news! I'm going to take responsibility for my part of this management relationship. I know you are busy. I know you are under a lot of pressure. I'm going to help you by getting a bunch of work done very well, very fast, all day long. I'm going to work with you to make sure I understand exactly what you expect of me. On every task, I'm going to break big deadlines into smaller, concrete performance benchmarks. I'm going to learn standard operating procedures and use checklists. I'm going to keep track of everything I'm doing and exactly how I'm doing it. I'm going to help you monitor, measure, and document my performance every step of the way. I'm going to solve problems as soon as they occur, and if I come to you for your help, you'll know I really need you. I'm going to learn and grow and be able to take on more and more responsibility. Count on me. With your help, I'm going to be really valuable to you!"

It's okay to manage your boss. You just need to get really good at it.

CHAPTER TWO

The First Person You Have to Manage Every Day Is Yourself

You want to take charge of your role in every relationship with every boss. But let's face it. You are not in charge: your bosses—both formal and informal—are in charge.

They give you assignments often without much guidance. Maybe they say, "Just take a crack at it." But it's not up to you what to do—and you darn well know that. You have to beg whenever you need resources, including the training necessary to accomplish your tasks more effectively. You also may be held accountable for bottom-line numbers—numbers that are easy to measure, like quarterly profits in your region—that have little to do with measuring your performance yet directly affect your ranking and pay. Meanwhile, you have more work on your plate than you have time to complete in a day, week, or month. Various bosses make competing demands on your time without communicating with each other. And some bosses have raging tempers that you do not want to cross.

Problems are mounting all around you, but you don't have the time or the authority to deal with them. You want to raise the alarm and scream out, "Things are *not* okay!" But raising alarms is frowned on in your organization. People are expected to stay positive and deal with their own problems.

So many factors are beyond your control at work. I've done hundreds of focus groups with people to find out what gets in the way of their success at work. Predictably, nine out of ten responses are factors that are totally beyond the control of the individual:

- Company policies, rules, regulations, culture, and standard operating procedures
- The way things have always been done around here
- Too much work and not enough time
- Too many low-priority activities that take me away from my most important tasks and responsibilities
- Conflict between and among employees, which creates a stressful, negative mood
- Resources are limited, and sometimes I don't have the people, material, and tools that I need to do the job
- No clear chain of command in this organization
- I answer to too many different people
- My various bosses have different standards of performance and conduct, and conflicting understandings of the rules and policies, and of what takes priority
- Some bosses yell and scream and make things difficult
- Managers don't make time for one-on-one discussions with me, make expectations clear, keep track of my performance, or give me honest, constructive feedback

Blame, blame, blame. Don't get me wrong. These are all real challenges that get in the way of your success at work. There is only one problem: when you focus your attention on factors outside your own control, you are by definition powerless. If you want to be powerful, then you need to focus on the one factor you can always control: you.

You have limited time, but you can gain control of your time enough to take charge of yourself every day. You can play an active role in managing your part of your relationship with every boss. You can make sure you understand what is expected of you; what your concrete goals are; what guidelines and schedule you need to follow. You can get your hands on necessary resources or work around a resource gap. You can keep track of your own performance and make work a rewarding experience for yourself, even if you can't get the pay and work conditions you'd really like. Ultimately, you can decide how you are going to operate with every single person at work, from the most interesting and highly engaged coworker to the loudest, meanest jerk.

How? First, make sure that the first person you manage every day is yourself. Make sure you are taking good care of yourself outside of work so that you are bringing your very best to work. And while you are at work, you should be all about the work. Your work, that is. Focus on playing the role assigned to you before you ever try to reach beyond that role. And before you even attempt to manage your boss, you need to do the following:

1. Figure out where you fit in your organization or department.

2. Bring your best self to work every day.

3. Make sure you are not the jerk at work.

4. Be a great workplace citizen.

5. Get lots of work done very well, very fast, every day.

6. Be a problem-solver, not a complainer.

7. Anticipate and avoid problems.

8. Regularly assess your productivity, the quality of your work, and your behavior.

Focus on controlling *you*. You cannot ignore all those factors outside yourself, which define the context of your situation, wherever you find yourself. But you can control what you do within the context of your job and work situation. The first step is to figure out where you fit within this context.

FIGURE OUT WHERE YOU FIT IN YOUR ORGANIZATION

No matter who you are, what you want to achieve, or how you want to behave, your role in any work situation is determined in large part by factors that have nothing to do with you. Every situation has a context that limits possibilities and limits the scope of your potential role.

To get a handle on the factors that determine your work situation and role, you need to ask yourself: Where am I, or what is this workplace like? What is going on here, or what is the mission of the group? Who are these people, or what role does each person play in the organization? Why are they here, or what is at stake for each person in the group? How are they accustomed to doing things here, or what are the "standard operating procedures" (both formal and informal) of this organization?

Once you get a handle on the context of your work situation, you have to ask yourself where you fit in this context. Why are you here? What is at stake for you? When did you get here? What is your appropriate role in relation to the other people in the group? What is your appropriate role in relation to the mission? What expectations and hopes are reasonable for you to have?

When you have really come to understand your role in any work context, then your number one responsibility is to play that role to the absolute best of your ability. That means contributing your very best and putting in more time and effort, no matter how lowly, mundane, or repetitive your tasks and responsibilities might seem in relation to the overall mission of your organization.

BRING YOUR BEST SELF TO WORK EVERY DAY

Attitude matters, a lot. Effort, too, matters—a lot.

Let me give you an example why attitude and effort count for so much. Over the years I've been honored to work with many fine people throughout the branches of the United States Armed Forces. Recently, I spent time with the crew of an important military aircraft. One of the crew member duties in missions (which last as long as ten hours) is to lie facedown in a window facing the ground in order to provide visual confirmation of the aircraft's electronic surveillance of the ground below. "Basically, I just lie down there with my eyes wide open and focused," the young airman told me. "We have very advanced systems on the plane, but I am the eyeballs. I need to provide visual [confirmation] to make sure we don't fire on any [friendly forces] or civilians. But I also am watching for muzzle flares, which might indicate enemy forces." Of critical importance, this young airman is also looking for enemy fire directed at the plane: "When we are fired on, we only have a few seconds to detect that and take countermeasures to protect the plane."

As I talked with this young airman, I couldn't help but compare him with the many people who have complained to me that their jobs are lowly, mundane, or repetitive. For hours at a time, he stays focused and blinks as little as possible. During a ten-hour mission, there might be only a handful of incidents of which the airman would actually need to take notice, and take action on. I asked the airman whether it's sometimes hard to stay alert on the job. "Sir, I don't have a choice," he responded. "The difference between me giving 99 percent or 110 percent could be the difference between life or death for me, for people on the ground, and for my crew."

The crew numbered thirteen. Each person played a narrow, focused role, and each was critical to the safety and effective operation of the airplane and its mission. And every one of them knew that they had no choice but to give 110 percent all the time because the performance of every role was a life-or-death matter.

For your sake, I hope that every move you make at work is not a life-or-death matter. Still, if you want to succeed, you would do well to follow that young airman's example. No matter how narrow or mundane or lowly or repetitive you might find your current role, play that role to the max. If you really want to grow, you need to bring your very best effort and very best attitude to work every day.

That's easier said than done, right?

A lot of theories are out there about how to be your best at work. Let me take a quick look at the leading ideas:

Play to your strengths at work. Working primarily on tasks and responsibilities that you enjoy and are particularly good at is great advice and would surely take some of the stress out of work. The problem is that most of us don't have the luxury to mostly do work that we enjoy and are good at. The real challenge is, how do you keep doing good work day after day—and feel good about it—when the work is not necessarily work that you enjoy or excel at?

Balance your time at work with free time. Resting, recovering, relaxing, and rejuvenating is also great advice. But most of us simply don't have enough time to do everything we need to do each day, at work and outside of work. The real challenge is, how do you stay focused and energetic when you barely have time to think, much less rest?

Work with people you like and respect. Avoiding people you find "toxic" and sticking to those you enjoy working with is great advice. The problem is that very few people can choose their coworkers, subordinates, bosses, vendors, and customers. You work with the people you work with. The challenge is, how do you maintain your equilibrium and equanimity when you have to deal with so many people whom you probably would not choose as your colleagues?

Work in a workspace that is comfortable and in a location that you enjoy. If only! Again, the real challenge is, how do you stay upbeat and strong if you are physically uncomfortable at work and stuck in a location that is not your preference?

Leave your nonwork issues at the door when you arrive at work. As good advice as that may be, it's just not realistic. If things are adrift in your life outside of work, then you will be distracted by those concerns, whether you are at work or at home. Sometimes you need to attend to your outside life from work, just as you sometimes need to attend to work matters from home. The boundaries between work and nonwork are no longer very clear in today's always connected 24/7 world.

If you are like most people, you probably struggle some days: you feel tired or your morale might be dampened. Before you can do your best every day at your job, *you* need to *be* at your best. That means you need to take good care of yourself both inside and outside of work.

You need to care for three elements for *you* to stay healthy. I sometimes walk seminar participants through the following reality check. I call it the "best-self reality check":

> *Are you taking good care of your mind?* What are the main sources of input for your mind right now? How can you expose your mind to a greater variety of input?
>
> *Are you taking good care of your body?* When do you sleep? What do you put into your body? How do you exercise?
>
> *Are you taking good care of your spirit?* Do you know what you believe? What is your purpose? What is your attitude? How can you improve your attitude?

Being at your best and bringing your best attitude to work also means cultivating high quality, high integrity, and adaptability. You are what you say, do, and create. No matter how grand your intentions or how generous and kind you may be, others will know you only by your words, actions, and creations.

Be of high quality. Always hold yourself to a high standard. Then go for it. Don't let yourself be paralyzed by the myth of "100 percent." Most people can accomplish 98 percent of almost any undertaking quickly and efficiently. If you ask me, 98 percent is the highest standard of quality attainable by human beings. I'm not saying that avoidable errors should be excused. The 2 percent I am talking about is the central character in the myth proliferated by procrastinators and "failurephobes" (the myth is that they get nothing done because they are actually perfectionists). That 2 percent is so intangible that it's just not worth agonizing over, not for even five minutes. So hold yourself to the highest standard attainable (98 percent), and go for it.

Be full of integrity. If anyone wants you to lie, cheat, steal, or harm others, don't do it. Quit if necessary. Blow the whistle if you think it's appropriate. No matter what, don't get involved in unethical dealings. It's not worth any price. Be honest, and honest people will gravitate toward you. But let's face it, that's the easy part. How much effort is required to reject downright dishonesty and corruption? Real integrity requires proactive behavior: it requires breaking your back to deliver when people are counting on you; helping others even when nobody is there to give you credit; intervening when others are being treated unfairly; and speaking out loud for unpopular causes you believe in.

Be adaptable. People who are too attached to the way things are have a hard time learning new skills, performing new tasks, doing old tasks in new ways, working with new machines, new managers, new coworkers, new customers, new rules, or no rules. Usually, the greatest difficulty for such people is the uncertainty—not knowing what lies just around the corner. Don't be one of these people. Learn to love change. Master today's changes and tomorrow's uncertainty, because things are going to keep changing, faster and faster, with or without you. Bringing your best self to work means being one of the few people who is willing to do whatever is needed, whenever it's needed, whether it is something you already know how to do or not; whether it is supposed to be "your job" or not; whether it is something you love to do or something you are just going to have to tolerate for a few weeks or months.

MAKE SURE YOU ARE NOT THE JERK AT WORK

Often in my seminars I use the example of a small software company I've worked with, which gained some notoriety in the late 1990s for its "no jerks" policy. Meant to capture some of the intangibles of interpersonal relationships, the policy prohibited employees from "acting like a jerk."

What usually ensues in my seminars is a lively discussion about what it means to act like a jerk at work. Most seminar participants agree that it's pretty easy to know when somebody else is acting like a jerk—we know it when we see it. The real challenge is figuring out when you are the one acting like a jerk.

How do you know? You know you are acting like a jerk at work if you

- Approach relationships from the vantage point of what you want or need from others rather than what you have to offer the other person.

- Blame others and make excuses when things go wrong rather than focus on the role you played in creating the problem and on what you can do to contribute to the solution.

- Take yourself seriously but don't always take your obligations seriously.

- Tease and make fun of others or call them names.
- Interrupt when others are speaking or don't pay close attention when others are speaking.
- Make negative personal observations about individuals.
- Hold strong opinions about the work product of another individual but never articulate your thoughts in a constructive manner.
- Focus on the negative aspects of situations without volunteering to help make things better.
- Deny, steal, or begrudge credit for the success of others.
- Lose your temper or raise your voice, even if you are only "talking to yourself."

If you find yourself doing any of these things, well, now you know: *You* might be acting like a jerk at work. If you are, it's going to hold you back. Mark my words.

If that's you, knock it off.

People with good interpersonal skills and who are conscientious in their interactions with others are much more successful. How do you develop "good interpersonal skills" and "conscientious interactions"?

Approach every relationship by staying focused on what you have to offer the other person. First, define the value you want to add—now or within a reasonable period of time—in this relationship. Until you define the value you are willing and able to add in any situation, it will be impossible to sell that value to anyone else.

Be a model of trust. Take personal responsibility for everything you say and do, hold yourself accountable, and never make excuses when you make a mistake. If you make a mistake, just apologize and make every effort to fix it.

Remove your ego. Don't take yourself too seriously, but always take your commitments and responsibilities seriously. Extend personal vulnerability, but never undermine your own credibility.

Listen carefully. Never interrupt or let your mind wander when others are speaking. Stay focused on what the other person is saying. When it's your turn, ask open-ended questions first and respond directly only after you are confident you understand what the other person is saying or the other's point of view.

Empathize. Always try to imagine yourself in the other person's position. Ask yourself what thoughts and feelings you might have if you were in that person's place. Then behave in a way and say the kinds of things that you would appreciate hearing under the same circumstances.

Exhibit respect and kindness. Take courtesy the extra mile. If you think the other person is pressed for time, be brief. If you think something might be wrong, ask if there is anything you can do to help (but don't be pushy). Never share observations that might be insulting, and never hesitate to share a compliment.

Speak up and make yourself understood. If you don't say what's on your mind, you'll have no chance of connecting with people, getting them to share your interests, influencing their thoughts, or persuading them to follow your way. Of course, sometimes it helps to take a quiet moment and clarify, for yourself, what really is on your mind. If it's something that ought to be shared, take an extra moment to think about the most effective words and actions to get your message across.

Be a motivator. Visualize positive results. Be enthusiastic and share your positive vision. Never speak of a problem unless you have thought of at least one potential solution.

Celebrate the success of others. Always give people credit for their achievements, no matter how small. And go out of your way to catch people doing things right.

BE A GREAT WORKPLACE CITIZEN

Every workplace is different. One of the most impressive organizations I've ever worked with is a restaurant chain that has an enterprise-wide rule: "Closed Sundays"! Since this restaurant chain functions as a franchise, where each restaurant operation has an ownership stake in the revenues of its restaurant, the "Closed Sundays" policy means every restaurant operator loses one-seventh of the restaurant's potential revenue every week (probably more because it's a weekend). Of course, when they sign on, the restaurant operators agree to that sacrifice. As one leader on the corporate side of the organization told me, "That's just who we are. That's our identity. It's central to our values. If you don't like that we are closed Sundays, there are probably going to be a lot of other things about us that you don't like either."

In fact, the entire culture of this organization is wrapped around a set of traditional, conservative values. Indeed, it would be very difficult to succeed in this organization if you didn't share those values. Not because the organization would discriminate against you. Rather, you just wouldn't fit in or feel comfortable there. It would be like taking a vow of poverty and then going to work at Goldman Sachs. Why would anyone do that?

What does this mean for you? First, it means you need to know what matters to you on a deep level. Know what you believe. Know what you can't support or can't stand for. Second, you need to understand the culture and values of your organization. If you are feeling out of place at work, perhaps a values disconnect might be responsible. In many organizations, the values and culture are not so obvious; they are generally composed of two elements: the written rules, namely, the mission statement, code of conduct, rules, and regulations; and the unwritten rules, the unspoken rules that dictate "how things get done around here."

Finally, once you identify the culture and values, make sure you can get on board and become a good workplace citizen. Ask yourself whether you will feel good, or at least feel comfortable, contributing to this workplace? Can you succeed here? If you are out of sync with the culture and values of your organization, you will have a very hard time succeeding in that organization: If you are a dedicated anarchist, then you shouldn't be working for the IRS. If you refuse to wear a uniform, then you shouldn't be a police officer. If you don't believe in eating meat, then you shouldn't go to work at a steakhouse.

Don't get me wrong. I'm not suggesting that you embrace and adopt an organization's values and culture as your own if you don't agree with them. I'm only suggesting that if you can't get in sync, then you should be planning your exit.

By the way, although every organization is different, when it comes to being a good workplace citizen there are some good old-fashioned standards of conduct by which you can almost never go wrong. To wit:

- Be on time, or a little bit early.
- Don't take long breaks.
- Don't leave early, and even stay a little late sometimes.
- Underpromise and overdeliver.

- Don't badmouth others, and try not to speak of others unless they are present.
- Keep your word.
- Keep confidences.
- Be an accurate source of information.
- Don't keep other people waiting.
- Overdress rather than underdress.
- Practice old-fashioned good manners, saying, please, thank you, you're welcome, excuse me, I'm sorry, and if appropriate, addressing people as Mr., Ms., Doctor, Professor, and so on.

GET LOTS OF WORK DONE
VERY WELL, VERY FAST, EVERY DAY

You knock yourself out every day giving 110 percent to your job. You have good relationships at work. Yet despite your best efforts, it feels like your work is just not good enough. The quality of your work is not what it should be, or your productivity is too low. You just aren't getting enough work done, and done well, given the time you spend on it. Every day, I hear from talented, hardworking people in the real world who are scrambling to get more work done better and faster, but they are still not getting the results they need.

Take this example of a talented professional who is now about to become a partner at a medium-sized consulting firm. But it almost didn't turn out that way. He has impeccable credentials and had acquired significant experience in one of the bigger consulting firms in his field before landing a job at his current medium-sized firm.

"When I first started working at [the current company],
I was like a fish out of water," he shared with me. "There was
much less structure to the work than I was used to from my
years working at [the bigger firm]. . . . At [the bigger firm], I
would work with a pretty good-sized team on a client engagement for months at a time. Everyone was expected to maintain
their individual work plan and schedule of deliverables. We
had checklists to guide us through the work to make sure we
were following the procedures. We had a team meeting at the
beginning of each week where each of us would go through our
key priorities and our to-do lists for the week.

"At the new firm, there was much less structure. The client
engagements were smaller, and it was common to get pulled off
of one client matter and thrown onto something else entirely
for a while. Depending on who was in charge of a particular
client engagement, there would or wouldn't be an overall work
plan. So it was a lot harder to keep my priorities straight and
stay organized and focused." In that less structured setting, he
continued, "I was having a really hard time being as productive as I was used to being. I kept finding I was going in the
wrong direction on one thing or another, sometimes for days
at a time, before I realized it. I was getting to work earlier and
staying later, but I was wasting time, working a lot more hours
than I ever had, but impressing nobody."

The situation kept getting worse until he had a long heart-
to-heart conversation with one of the partners: "He basically
told me, 'Look, I've been there. I know exactly what you are
going through. You are used to having a lot more structure.
Here nobody gives you that structure. You have to create that
structure around your own work for yourself.'"

The lesson? "I realized I was going to have to get organized
and start making better use of my time. I was going to have to

develop good habits to keep track of my own work and maintain my focus. I had to set and keep track of my own priorities, work plan, schedule, to-do list, checklists for quality control. That helped a lot. It was pretty much the turnaround moment that made it possible for me to do as well as I've done here."

Eureka!

If you find yourself in a similar scenario—working hard but still not being as effective as you should—then you might reconsider your work habits, specifically your habits related to organization and focus. Regardless of where you work or what you do, if you are going to get lots of work done very well, very fast, day after day, you need structure and good habits:

Use your time wisely. There are 168 hours in a week. How do you use them? Most people waste endless hours without ever realizing they are doing so. Keep track of your time so you can eliminate time-wasters and stay focused on key priorities. One of the best gifts you can give yourself is maintaining an old-fashioned time log to understand how you are using your time and to identify and eliminate time-wasters. Each time you change from one activity to another, note it briefly in your log. Here's an example:

7:00 A.M.	Sat down at my desk, read over to-do list, set priorities for the day
7:10 A.M.	Got up to use bathroom and get coffee
7:45 A.M.	Sat back down at desk, opened e-mail
8:30 A.M.	Started preparing response to e-mail from manager
8:40 A.M.	Incoming phone call from Friend Smith
9:15 A.M.	Continued preparing response to e-mail from manager
9:25 A.M.	Got up to use bathroom and get another cup of coffee

The time log is useful only if you faithfully record every activity precisely. Used properly, three or four days is all it takes to get a reality check on how you are spending your time and when you are wasting it.

Set priorities and revisit them regularly. If you have limited time and too much to do, then you need to set priorities—an order of precedence or preference for your tasks—so that you control what gets done first, second, third, and so on. Make sure you are devoting the lion's share of your time to first and second priorities. When it comes to setting day-to-day priorities, postpone low-priority activities until high-priority activities are well ahead of schedule.

Plan your work every step of the way, but be prepared to adjust as needed. Before you can make a realistic work plan, you have to know how long each task is actually going to take. Break big projects into manageable tasks; estimate accurately how long each will take to complete; and set a timetable based on those realistic estimates. Of course, no matter how great the plan, you will always be subject to interruptions. Emergencies and distractions always spring up and disrupt a perfect plan. Don't be thrown off. Pay close attention and be prepared to revise and adjust your plans every step of the way.

Take notes, maintain a to-do list, and create and refer to checklists. Note-taking is a process. If you take notes every step of the way at work, then you can use them to maintain your to-do list, to track progress, and to revise and adjust your work plan as needed. Also use your note-taking to create checklists to help you ensure quality and completeness of your work. Checklists are common in workplaces where there is little room for error: operating rooms, airplane cockpits, nuclear weapons launch sites, accounting firms, and so on. There's a reason for that! Checklists are powerful tools. No matter where you work or what you do, taking notes and rigorously using to-do lists and checklists to guide you will cause your error rates to go down, quality to go up, and assignments to be completed on time.

Take action and keep moving forward. Nothing gets done unless somebody does it. In this case, that somebody is you. If you have one hundred phone calls to make, you start with the first one and move on to the second, and then the third, and so on. Each call is a concrete action. Every concrete action can be broken down into smaller components, and each small component is itself another concrete action. If you get bogged down with the feeling that you are "not getting anything done," break every task into its smaller components and start tackling them one at a time. You will start moving forward.

BE A PROBLEM-SOLVER, NOT A COMPLAINER

No matter how great your work, your colleagues, or your organization may be, problems are a part of everyday reality in every workplace. Mostly these problems are not of your own making. But you still have to deal with them or else suffer the consequences.

Often when I talk about being a problem-solver, people in my seminars start grumbling. Two major themes emerge: it's easy to identify problems, but you aren't in a position to solve most of them; and most of the time, when you go to your boss to point out the problem, your report is treated as an unwelcome complaint.

Does any of this sound familiar? When I say, "be a problem-solver," this is what I mean:

First, decide whether the problem is an emergency. Ask yourself a series of questions: What harm could occur if the problem continues unresolved? Is time of the essence in order to prevent the harm from occurring? To whom should I report this? This is sort of like deciding whether to call 911. It is dangerous and irresponsible to try to solve certain kinds of problems on your own, no matter how able and confident you may be. Be alert to emergencies and know who to call, how to call, and what to say in the event of a true emergency. But don't call 911 lightly. If the problem is not an emergency, then reporting it as such will give the impression that you are delivering an unwelcome complaint.

Second, if you've determined the problem is not an emergency, then decide whether you can fix it and create a plan for solving it. Then do a quick reality check: is this a solution you can implement without permission or input from someone else? If so, then solve the problem and keep a record of it. If you need somebody to give you permission to solve the problem, then move on to the next step.

Third, take your plan to fix the problem to your boss or the person responsible.

Of course, the most common problems you will encounter in the workplace will probably not be emergencies or complaints or anything special, for that matter. They are usually small mistakes that occur while you are doing your job. No problem is so small that it should be left alone; small problems too often fester and grow into bigger problems. When you diagnose a problem, start focusing intensely on implementing concrete solutions.

If you are talking with your bosses on a regular basis, then talking about small problems—whatever they may be—should be something you do as a matter of course. Addressing one small problem after another is what ongoing continuous performance improvement is all about.

ANTICIPATE AND AVOID PROBLEMS

The real trick is learning to anticipate and avoid one problem after another. That requires judgment. Good judgment is the ability to see the connection between cause and effect. It allows you to project likely outcomes or accurately predict the consequences of your decisions and actions. The single most important factor in developing good judgment is getting in the habit of thinking ahead and playing out the likely sequence of moves and countermoves before making a move. If you take this decision or action, who is likely to respond, and how, when, where, and why? What set of options will this create? What set of options will this cut off? How will it play out if you take another decision or action instead?

To jump-start your development of good judgment, try using the following decision and action tool to scrutinize each of your decisions:

What decision was made? Who made it? Why? What was the outcome?

DECISIONS?	WHO?	WHY?	OUTCOME?

What actions were taken? Who made them? Why? What was the outcome?

ACTIONS?	WHO?	WHY?	OUTCOME?

What were the leading alternative decisions that were not made? What different outcomes might have occurred?

ALTERNATIVE DECISIONS?   POSSIBLE DIFFERENT OUTCOMES?

What were the leading alternative actions that were not taken? What different outcomes might have occurred?

ALTERNATIVE ACTIONS?   POSSIBLE DIFFERENT OUTCOMES?

REGULARLY ASSESS YOUR PRODUCTIVITY, THE QUALITY OF YOUR WORK, AND YOUR BEHAVIOR

Rigorous self-evaluation is the beginning, middle, and end of self-management. It is the essential habit of self-improvement. Constantly assess your own productivity, the quality of your work, and your behavior. Be honest with yourself and make a commitment to constant, rigorous self-evaluation.

Continuously ask yourself these questions:

Productivity: What can I do to get more work done faster? Should I revisit my priorities? Do I need to focus my time better? How can I eliminate time-wasters? Do I need better time budgets? Do I need to make better plans?

Quality: Am I working within the guidelines and specifications for my tasks and responsibilities? Do I need to
make better use of checklists? Do I need to start adding
some bells and whistles to my work product?

Behavior: What can I do to be a better workplace citizen?
Can I eliminate any substandard behaviors? Can I start
adding any superstar behaviors? How can I take more
initiative without overstepping my bounds?

Self-evaluation is an engine of self-improvement only if you
use the information you've learned from it. Start with one small
goal—the smaller the better. Once you meet that goal, take another small step. Self-management and self-improvement come
one small step at a time. It's a never-ending process because
there is always room to improve.

○ ○

Once you have *yourself* under control, you can focus on managing your boss. But you have to stay focused: no matter how
thoroughly and diligently you practice the techniques of self-
management, once in a while you are likely to fall off the
wagon. What do you do when this happens? Bounce back. Get
back to practicing the basics of self-management. Get back to
work and do better.

First manage yourself. Next you can manage your boss.

CHAPTER THREE

Get in the Habit of Managing Your Bosses Every Day

If you are like most employees, you probably juggle several projects, tasks, and responsibilities for several bosses—usually a boss that you report to and several informal ones, such as team leaders, heads of departments that work closely with yours, or even your boss's boss. You get lots of seemingly urgent e-mails and voicemails from Mr. Remote, a boss who works across town. They come whenever anything relating to your project pops into his head. You get just as many urgent e-mails from another boss, Ms. Email, who works across the hall from you. The worst interruptions, however, come from Mr. Nervous, who constantly looks over your shoulder. Of course, the one boss with whom you need to talk urgently has been unavailable for days, despite your concerned calls and e-mails; then all of a sudden Ms. Unavailable comes whirling into your workspace in "crisis mode." After solving the problem, Ms. Unavailable declares, "Now I'm really behind on my work," signaling that she will be unavailable again for the foreseeable future—unless something else goes terribly wrong.

Are you spending too much time dealing with your bosses? It might seem like that. But very likely the reality is exactly the opposite. The problem is not that you are spending too much time with bosses, but rather that you are not spending enough time dealing with them in the right way. As I discussed in Chapter One, most managers and nonmanagers alike are so busy juggling their various responsibilities that they don't usually make time for regular management conversations. Instead, most management conversations occur ad hoc, maybe during group meetings—even if many of the people present at the meeting don't need to be part of that conversation—in sudden e-mails and voicemails, in passing, or when there is a big problem that desperately needs attention.

I call this phenomenon "management on the fly" or "management by special occasion." In this sort of management there is no systematic logic to the timing of conversations; in fact, they are random, incomplete, and often too late to avoid a problem or solve one before it grows large.

The only alternative to being subjected to management on the fly and management by special occasion is for *you* to get in the habit of having regular one-on-one management conversations with every boss you answer to. The hard part is actually getting in the habit of making time every day to manage your bosses. New behaviors, no matter how good they are, often don't feel comfortable until they become habits. It will take time to get used to the new behaviors, not just for you but also for the bosses you are going to be managing more closely.

After you've built more effective boss-managing habits, you'll still have to deal with unexpected problems, but they won't be the kinds of problems that could have been avoided.

And you'll still have to face plenty of difficult challenges when dealing with your bosses. But your working relationships with them will be in such good shape that you'll be able to handle those challenges effectively with confidence and skill.

So take the initiative. Schedule regular one-on-one management meetings with your bosses.

WHEN, HOW OFTEN, AND FOR HOW LONG?

How often you should meet with your boss or bosses depends partly on the nature of the work you are engaged in with each of them. How often you should meet with a particular manager will also be determined by his or her particular style and preferences and also by what works for you. In an ideal world, maybe you would talk with every single boss—reviewing your work and getting set up for success that day—every day. Some bosses need more attention than others. But talking to every boss every day is not always possible and may not be ideal.

In fact, every situation is different, but most of the time the short answer is that you should be meeting one on one with each boss more often than you are currently. You should meet more often with a boss if you are working with this boss

- For the first time
- On a new project
- On a project with especially high stakes
- On a project where there is a lot of uncertainty

The last thing in the world you want to do is make bad use of a boss's time by meeting more often than necessary or by wasting time during those meetings. Keep your management conversations brief, straightforward, and to the point. As long as you conduct these one-on-one conversations regularly, there is no reason they should be long and convoluted. The goal is to make them focused, efficient, brief, and simple. Prepare in advance so that you can move the conversation along swiftly. Once you've gotten into a routine with each boss, fifteen minutes every week or every other week should be all you need. Like everything else, it's a moving target. Over time, you'll have to gauge how much time you need to spend with each boss.

If things are not going well on a particular assignment, consider meeting with your boss every day for a while. Don't make the mistake of spending hours on tearful inquisitions, indictments, or confessions. Keep these meetings short and consistent. Chances are strong that things are not working out because you are not getting enough guidance, direction, and support. Once you spend more time with your boss talking through the work you are doing, you are likely to work through solutions to 99 percent of problems.

If things are going very well with your work, do you need to spend fifteen minutes every day or even every week with your boss? Maybe you need to meet only every other week. But if you don't spend at least that much time with that boss, then you won't actually know whether things are going as well as you think they are. All you really know is that no problems have come up on your radar screen or the boss's radar screen. Spend those fifteen minutes verifying that things are indeed going as well as you think they are. And if in fact they are, then you still need to work with your boss to find out if you can make things go even better.

You'll be shocked how much you can get done in fifteen minutes. Take any boss you have not spoken with in detail for a while. Spend fifteen minutes with that boss asking probing questions about the details of your work, and you will find some surprises. You'll be darn glad you had that conversation. And you should be in a hurry to have another one.

Don't forget to consider what day and time is best to meet with each boss. With some bosses you may be able to schedule regular meetings at fixed days and times. But if your boss has an irregular schedule, then the best practice is to finish each conversation with that boss by scheduling the next one.

Exactly how often, for how long, and when you meet with your boss is likely to be a moving target. You will have to evaluate your situation on an ongoing basis and adjust as necessary. One way or another, you can't wait around to be managed on the fly or by special occasion anymore.

WHAT SHOULD YOU TALK ABOUT IN ONE-ON-ONES?

The fundamental goal of one-on-one meetings is communicating with your boss about the work you are doing for him or her. Over time, you and your boss will use your growing knowledge of each other to guide you during each conversation. But generally you'll talk about the work and whether it is going well, poorly, or just fine. Maintain an ongoing dialogue with every boss about the four management basics:

- What is expected of you.
- The resources you need to meet those expectations.
- Honest feedback on your performance and guidance on how to adjust it as necessary.
- What credit and reward you will earn for your hard work.

With each boss, you will have to decide what to focus on and discuss at each one-on-one. Before your meetings, you should ask yourself the following: Are there problems that haven't been spotted yet? Problems that need to be solved? Resources that need to be obtained? Are any instructions or goals not clear? Has anything happened since you and your boss last talked that the boss should know about? Are there questions that need to be answered by your boss?

At the very least, in these one-on-ones you need to receive updates on your progress. Get input from your boss while you have the chance. And think about the input you should be providing to the boss on what you are learning on the front line. Strategize together. Try to get a little advice, support, motivation, and yes, even inspiration once in a while.

TEAM MEETINGS ARE NO
SUBSTITUTE FOR ONE-ON-ONES

Some managers favor team meetings over one-on-one management conversations, but team meetings are no substitute for your regular, individual check-ins. When you meet with the boss and look her in the eye, clarify expectations, offer an account of your performance, push for candid, constructive feedback, there's no place for either of you to hide. In a team meeting, however, it's easy for both of you to hide.

Maybe the boss feels more comfortable sharing difficult news or providing feedback to the whole team than talking directly to each of its members. The problem is, the difficult news or feedback is often aimed at only one or two people. If the criticism is meant for you, wouldn't you rather have that conversation in private? If it's not meant for you, then don't you have a lot more to do than listen in on what should be a one-on-one between that boss and a colleague?

How often have you sat through a team meeting waiting for just one granule of information that you needed to hear? How many times have you attended one of these meetings hoping against hope that you might get an update you need; get a chance to raise a critical issue; get answers to important questions; or otherwise receive guidance and direction? The reality is that it's a whole lot harder to get your boss to tune in to you and your work in a meaningful way in a team meeting. Sometimes the best thing that results from a team meeting is the opportunity to catch your boss for a spontaneous one-on-one huddle immediately following the meeting.

Team meetings serve a purpose. They are ideal for sharing information with the whole group and are often necessary to bring people that work interdependently together to hear about what everyone is doing, what issues are coming up in their projects, and so on. Inevitably, you will attend more than your share of team meetings. How can you make the most of them?

Before attending any meeting or presentation, make sure you know what the meeting is about and whether your attendance is required. Identify your role in the meeting: What information are you responsible for gathering or communicating? Prepare in advance: Should you review or read any material before the meeting? Do you need to have any conversations before the meeting? If you are making a presentation, prepare even more. Ask yourself exactly what value you have to offer the group. If you are not a primary actor in the meeting, often the best thing you can do is to say as little as possible and practice good meeting manners. If you are tempted to speak up, ask yourself whether everyone needs to hear this point right here and now? If you have a question, could it be asked at a later time, off-line? Remember, some meetings are a waste of time. Try not to say a single word that will unnecessarily lengthen such a meeting.

More important, don't fool yourself. No matter how much of your boss's time you get in team meetings, they are no substitute for one-on-one management conversations with your boss. One-on-ones are where all the action is.

WHEN YOUR BOSS DOESN'T HAVE ENOUGH TIME FOR ONE-ON-ONES

Some bosses are absolutely convinced that they are too busy to meet with you. Or maybe they are convinced it's just not necessary and they simply do not want to meet with you.

If this is the case with your boss, you might have to do some convincing.

I hope this isn't the case, but if your boss seems resistant, remember that it's probably nothing personal. Stick to the business case. It's as simple as this: when you don't meet for regular one-on-one conversations, then the work you are doing becomes susceptible to:

- Unnecessary problems that are more likely to occur
- Small problems that could be solved easily but instead turn into bigger problems
- Resources that are less likely to be optimized and more likely to be wasted
- Lower productivity and quality, and diminished morale

When bosses hide in their offices or run from one meeting to another, they often leave a power vacuum on the day-to-day management front. Ringleaders sometimes emerge to fill the vacuum. Often these ringleaders are squeaky wheels who have good personal relationships with other employees, and assert their authority and influence in ways that are self-serving or even damaging to the team. Sometimes they form cliques, bully others, or spread rumors, but more often they are simply self-deceived mediocre performers who believe they are high-performers. They offer guidance, direction, and support to their coworkers, but they often lead people in the wrong direction. If a ringleader has filled the power vacuum left by your absent boss, it's more important than ever that you get your boss's attention so you can stay focused on the work and move in the right direction.

Remind your boss that he or she is likely to end up spending a lot of management time on you regardless. But if it doesn't happen up front in these one-on-ones, then it will probably be late in the process, after small problems that could have been avoided or solved sooner need his or her intervention. Make your one-on-one time "high-leverage" time, and your boss will know that it is worthwhile spending time with you.

No matter how convincing your arguments are, some bosses are still nearly impossible to pin down for a scheduled one-on-one. Maybe they are responsible for too many direct reports and feel they can't possibly talk to sixteen, sixty, or even more employees on a regular basis and still get their own work done. Or maybe they have erratic schedules, making your scheduling a meeting with them pointless. Such a boss might say, "If you want to catch me for a one-on-one, then you'll have to take me on the fly when I'm available."

What do you do?

One nurse working in a bustling hospital, who was effective at managing her boss, shared her simple technique for getting that incredibly busy boss's attention: stalking!

Here's what she told me: "My boss is responsible for forty-three nurses, technicians, and aides all reporting directly to her and nobody else. She is also responsible for a hospital annex in a different location. So it's pretty hard to get her attention." What does the nurse do to get her boss's attention? "I have a pretty good idea of her schedule and her M.O. I know what door she comes in and when, the route she takes to the locker room and to the cafeteria for coffee or to the vending machine for two Diet Cokes. When she has a free moment, I'm right there waiting for her. I've learned there are certain places and times when she really doesn't want me to try to talk to her, like when she is in the locker room. But there are other places and times when I know she will give me five, six, or seven minutes. It's not ideal, but I've gotten into a routine now of meeting with her while she gets her coffee in the morning or her Diet Coke in the afternoon. I prepare in advance with the issues and questions I need to run by her. I've got my pen and notebook, and I stand there taking notes."

What happens when the nurse and her boss are not working the same shifts? "Sometimes, if she is working the shift after me, I will wait and catch her on her way in. If she is working the shift before me, it's a bit harder because I haven't found the right time and place to get her on her way out the door. I guess I'll have to stalk her a bit more to figure out the best way to get her attention when she is leaving!"

What lessons can we learn from this nurse?

- Sometimes the best you can do is stage "spontaneous" one-on-one meetings.
- If you handle them right, you can turn ad hoc one-on-ones into regular meetings.

- Pay close attention to the boss's routine.

- Figure out where and when the boss does and does not want to have ad hoc meetings.

- Be prepared in advance for every staged "spontaneous" one-on-one.

- Keep the meetings focused and quick.

IF YOU OR YOUR BOSS WORK IN A REMOTE LOCATION

Some bosses are harder to stalk than others. You or your boss might work from home, at an office across town, or at a client location across the world. I've heard countless stories from very determined people who've had to stalk their bosses from remote locations, calling every fifteen minutes until the boss finally answers. Or texting; faxing; or Facebook-messaging. Or scheduling two-way web-cam conferences. Even showing up on-site at the boss's location to try to get some one-on-one time.

Again, I hope you are not in that situation.

The best situation is for you and your boss to work out a protocol for a regular schedule of one-on-one meetings whenever you can. Here are some best practices that you can apply if you don't work in the same location as your boss:

- Keep each other informed about when you'll both be at a central location, such as the organization's headquarters, so you can schedule in-person time.

- Schedule occasional in-person meetings when it is convenient for you to visit your boss in his or her remote location or when it is convenient for your boss to visit you where you work.

- If you have access to web-cams, schedule a regular one-on-one meeting via the web.

In the absence of in-person meetings and two-way web-cams, make good use of regular telephone conferences and various forms of electronic mail, such as instant messaging and e-mail. Unfortunately, too often when people communicate primarily via telephone and e-mail, they neglect to schedule regular one-on-one conversations, and as a result, their communications tend to be disorganized, incomplete, and random. Here are some best practices for using telephone and e-mail to communicate regularly with your boss:

- Schedule regular one-on-one telephone calls; then, honor those appointments.
- Prepare in advance of each one-on-one call. Send your boss an e-mail recapping what you've done since your last one-on-one, the steps that you've followed to get those things done, and any lingering questions or issues you have about those actions. Then outline what you plan to accomplish next, the steps you plan to follow, and any questions you may have about these upcoming actions.
- Ask your boss to respond to your e-mail in advance of your conversation to help you prepare even further by moving along an agenda item or adding other items.
- Send your boss a reminder via e-mail or text message thirty or sixty minutes before the scheduled conversation.
- Immediately following the call, send your boss an e-mail recapping what you both agreed on in your conversation: the actions you need to take, the steps you plan to

follow, the date and time of your next scheduled phone call, and a promise to send an agenda prior to the next meeting.

Sometimes when I teach these best practices in my seminars, someone will raise a hand and ask, "My boss works across the hall from me, but our entire relationship is conducted by telephone and e-mail. What should I do about that?" My view is that conducting face-to-face conversations—at least once in a while—is much better than conducting your management conversations solely by telephone and e-mail. I suggest following the same best practices I offer for employees and bosses who work at different locations. And, maybe once in a while, walk across the hall and try for a face-to-face meeting. You can poke your head in and ask, "Did you get that e-mail I just sent you?"

But if most of your communication is through telephone and e-mail, well, that's better than nothing. And there is an advantage: when you and your boss are communicating by e-mail, you are creating a paper (or electronic) trail. Save those e-mails, and you'll have a record of your ongoing dialogue with your boss about your work. If the e-mails are organized and thorough, then you might be able to use them for crafting work plans, schedules, to-do lists, checklists, and other tools to help guide you in your work.

If after attempting all these techniques your boss just won't give you any time whatsoever and remains absent, or unavailable, then he or she is a boss in name only. That boss is AWOL and negligent, and you have only three options:

1. Look for a new boss or job inside or outside your current organization.

2. Identify a worthy deputy of your AWOL boss—someone who is on the same team and has a little more experience, skill, or wisdom than you, or someone with more power or influence. Turn that worthy deputy into your de facto boss. Try building a routine of regular one-on-one meetings with him or her. Try reporting to the worthy deputy. Try clarifying expectations and getting support and guidance from the worthy deputy. You'd be amazed at how many worthy deputies take on de facto management relationships with good people who have been abandoned by AWOL bosses.

3. Sink or swim, but document and communicate your efforts every step of the way. Keep track in writing of every step you are planning to take each day and how you are planning to do it. Report your plans to your AWOL boss. Monitor and measure your progress in writing, and give a regular written account of your performance to your AWOL boss. Finally, offer frequently, in writing, to make yourself available for in-person one-on-ones with your AWOL boss. What else can you do?

WHAT ABOUT THE BOSS WHO HAS TOO MUCH TIME FOR YOU?

Until this point in the chapter, I have focused on the problem of not having enough one-on-one time with your bosses. But what if your boss wants to spend *too* much time with you?

Sometimes a boss who wants to spend too much time with you may simply be a "jerk boss." In Chapter Nine, I offer advice for dealing with these types of bosses. Often, though, bosses who take too much of your time are not being jerks; they just don't know any better. Sometimes I'm amazed by the stories people tell me of bosses who want to spend a bunch of time just shooting the breeze, or who want to be their employee's best friend, therapist, or mentor (or want *you* to be their mentor or therapist). Here's what to do if you have one of these bosses:

1. Talk about the work.

2. When anything other than the work is being discussed, don't talk.

3. When there is a break in the talking, go back to talking about the work.

4. Start taking notes every time the boss starts talking to you.

After a while of practicing these steps, if the problem persists, try adding these words: "Golly, I'm really pressed for time right now. I need to keep focusing on my work."

If your boss is great about meeting with you regularly but the meetings go on forever, make sure you bring an agenda (or provide it ahead of time) to the meeting to keep it focused on what you have done since the last meeting, and what you plan to do before the next one. Finally, you need a good strategy for ending your one-on-one meetings. Try this: when it's time to wrap up the meeting, show the notes you've taken during the meeting to the boss and say, "So this is what I'm going to do next." Then agree on a time and venue for your next one-on-one meeting.

If you have a boss who wants to meet too often, you need to develop a relationship of trust and confidence with that manager by quickly building a track record of fulfilled commitments. At first, meet as often as your boss requests. At each meeting, spell out a set of clearly defined goals and promise to deliver on them by the next meeting. Then deliver! Keep close track of your goals in writing, and monitor, measure, and document your achievements as you deliver on them. Start expanding on the process and make longer-term work plans that include schedules of goals and deadlines. Report regularly on your progress in writing to this manager. The strong likelihood is that it will become increasingly obvious to your boss that you two can meet less frequently.

The good news is that when managers manage too closely, you can usually help them realize it pretty quickly. When a manager works closely with you and watches you learn and grow over time, usually he or she will step back. No harm done. You need to help that boss practice the real art of empowerment: help him define for you the terrain—however limited—on which you have power; help her figure out the goals, guidelines, and timelines that are appropriate for you for each assignment.

Here's a simple rule: if you deliver on a small goal with a short deadline and meet all the specifications required for that assignment, then you can usually get your boss to delegate to you a more ambitious project (with a more ambitious deadline). As you demonstrate your proficiency, you can convince your boss to gradually increase the amount and importance of the work assigned to you—until you reach the appropriate scope of responsibility for you. Once you reach that point, focus your one-on-one meetings on getting an ongoing review of your work and how to improve it. Over time, you will be able to accept responsibility for even bigger, more complex projects, and your boss will learn to step back.

○ ○

I know you are busy. Your bosses are busy. Nobody has enough time.

That means you don't have time *not* to manage your bosses.

Dedicate time every day to managing your bosses, making it a rigorous habit. It will start to pay off almost immediately.

CHAPTER FOUR

Take It One Boss at a Time, One Day at a Time

You answer to so many people at work on a daily basis that sometimes it's hard to say exactly who your actual "boss" is. In many ways, clients and customers are your bosses. Colleagues in other departments who need things from you—so-called internal clients and customers—are also your bosses. And there are plenty of big shots at work, who may or may not interact with you daily but are obviously among your bosses: managers above you, or your boss's bosses; bosses on other shifts; bosses in and outside your areas; and bosses on your and other teams. Ultimately, you answer to all of these bosses.

Indeed, it helps to think of your relationships at work as customer relationships, and therefore as relationships in which you answer to these "customers" as if they were your bosses. After all, work consists of transactional relationships. You are getting paid a salary and maybe nonfinancial rewards, such as vacations or flexibility in your schedule, in exchange for your time and effort. If you are trying to do a great job at work every day, then you answer to everybody and try to please them all. When you do that, it inevitably results in competing—maybe conflicting—needs, expectations, requests, and demands on your time. You probably already have too much work on your plate from too many bosses. Plus, you need to keep straight the different work standards and management practices of each boss. That's a lot to balance and coordinate day after day.

Maybe you are fortunate enough to have relatively stable, clear, and orderly reporting relationships at work. You know exactly who your bosses are: you answer to boss A on project A. You answer to boss B on responsibility B. You answer to boss C on task C. With each boss, you have firmly established standards for the work and you have a routine for working together and for scheduling ongoing one-on-one management dialogues.

Or maybe you enjoy the rarest of cases: you answer to just one boss on all projects, responsibilities, and tasks. If you have just one boss, then congratulations! You will avoid the many frustrating complications that most people in the workplace face today. Remember, however, that all relationships are dynamic and changing. If your management relationship with your sole boss is of the very highest quality, then it's even more important that you maintain and grow it in the right direction.

No matter how many bosses—formal and informal—you answer to, your goal should be to maintain a high-quality management relationship with every one of them.

ESTABLISH A REGULAR, WELL-FUNCTIONING DIALOGUE WITH EVERY BOSS

Because every boss is different and has his or her own style, preferences, and habits when it comes to managing, the best way to a maintain a high-quality relationship with him or her is by establishing ground rules up front. At the outset of your relationship, have a conversation outlining how you are going to work together. Corporate or organizational policies are probably in place that already define some aspects of your working relationship. Clarify exactly where, when, and how you are going to observe and practice those policies whenever you are working on any task or project. Make a commitment to follow these practices, and then take responsibility for following through on them.

You also need to discuss up front some of the broader goals you have for working together, like maintaining certain levels of productivity and quality standards, making a valuable contribution, and achieving measurable results. You might even discuss subtle rules of conduct that are expected of you, such as work hours, attitude, attire, making personal calls at work, and so on.

But the most important thing you need to agree on from the get-go is how you plan to communicate with each other. Make sure you discuss scheduling regular ongoing conversations about work and confirm the following goals for every conversation: walking away with a mutual understanding of the goals of an assignment, spelling out guidelines and parameters, and specifying a clear timeline of deliverables. Suggest that you make a habit of asking each other clarifying questions and discussing step-by-step instructions for any new task. Finally, try to agree that you will each take notes and check at the end of each conversation that you are both on the same page.

CUSTOMIZE YOUR APPROACH TO EVERY BOSS

Your various bosses come to work with different backgrounds, personalities, styles, ways of communicating, work habits, motivations, levels of ability and skill, and accomplishment. Some of them are more engaged than others. One boss wants to spell out every detail for you, while another boss expects you to figure out everything on your own. In order to create the best working relationship with each boss, you must learn and understand how each boss works, and customize your approach for each of them accordingly.

I'm not suggesting that you cater to the whims of each boss or go happily along with downright bad management practices. But understanding a boss's whims and management weaknesses is not a bad thing. When you know the whims and weaknesses of a boss, then you have more tools in your kit of solutions with that manager. The only way to learn what works and what doesn't with each boss is to have those one-on-one management conversations. As you meet individually with each boss, the differences between bosses will jump right out at you. Over time, you'll be able to tune in to each boss and adjust your approach as needed. The best way to fine-tune your approach to each boss is to continually ask yourself six key questions:

1. Who is this boss at work?
2. Why do I need to manage this boss?
3. What do I need to talk about with this boss?

4. How should I communicate with this boss?

5. Where should I talk with this boss?

6. When should I talk with this boss?

Together, these questions make up a powerful tool for customizing your approach to each boss. I call it the "customizing lens," and I've used it to help tens of thousands of seminar participants tune in to their managers, their coworkers, and the employees they manage. If you become obsessed with asking and answering these questions, you won't be able to avoid customizing your approach with each boss.

1. Who Is This Boss at Work?

Don't worry. You don't need to ask yourself who this boss is deep inside—what her mind and spirit are like, or what her inner motivations might be. In fact, you shouldn't try. My view is that it's none of your business who this boss is deep inside, and you are probably not qualified to figure it out anyway. All you need to find out is who this boss is when it comes to work and managing.

You want to consider who she is at work so that you can adjust your approach accordingly. What is her position and reputation, and what are her responsibilities and other relationships? Is this boss in a very senior position or a relatively lower-level position? Does the boss handle very important work? Does the boss work alone most of the time, or is he involved in various task forces or teams? Does she meet with her bosses regularly? Are coworkers fond of her, or have you heard the boss badmouthed by others? This information will allow you to set expectations about your boss's overall time and energy, and to strategize the best way (how, when, and how long you should conduct your ongoing management conversations) to craft a strong, valuable relationship.

Another key aspect that you need to learn is who this boss is when it comes to managing. Is this boss a hardnose or is he easygoing? Calm or anxious? Detail-oriented or big picture? Brainiac or workhorse? Always here or never around? Hands-on or hands-off? Understanding how this boss works and manages will allow you to tailor how you communicate in your one-on-one conversations.

People often ask me how much they need to know about their boss's personal life. My answer is that you need to know enough to be polite. If you work together with anybody for any lengthy period of time, you might want to know something about their lives outside of work; for example, if that person is in a relationship or has kids. It would be a nice gesture if you remembered how many kids and their ages, roughly. It would be extra nice if you remembered their names. But that's usually enough. Focus on learning or remembering personal details about your boss's life that might bear on your working relationship with that boss. If your boss has newborn twins, you probably need to know that and be in tune with his peak productivity times. Maybe he is usually groggy and grumpy early in the morning; that is a bad time to meet with him. Or maybe it's exactly the opposite: he is up at 3 A.M. with the babies, so by the time you come in at 8, it's just before lunchtime for the boss—his best time to meet—and before his energy wanes.

Sometimes people ask me if they should try to share mutual interests with their boss in order to make friendly conversation. If the boss is a big fitness buff, should you take an interest in fitness too? Only if you want to get in shape. Your boss's interest in fitness, or anything else, is only relevant to you to the extent that it bears on your working relationship with that boss. So if your boss leaves the office to work out between 2 P.M. and 4 P.M., you probably need to know that she is unavailable during those hours, or that the best time to meet with her is just when she returns fresh from a five-mile run.

Maybe you are thinking, *Well, a boss with twin newborns or fitness fanatics are special cases, and probably don't apply to me.* Here's the truth: every boss is a special case. If you don't know what makes one of your bosses a special case, you need to find out as soon as possible.

2. Why Do I Need to Manage This Boss?

The key to answering this question is to have a clear understanding of your goals for managing each boss and of what you need from each boss. Ask yourself the following questions: Do I need to clarify expectations? Do I want to learn about the larger context in which my work fits in the overall mission of this organization? Do I need to get more concrete schedules for my deliverables? Do I want a comprehensive work plan or step-by-step instructions for achieving my tasks? Do I need a better understanding of the resources necessary and available to me to do my job? Do I need feedback on my progress? Do I need to make course corrections in my performance? Do I want credit for my hard work or to negotiate a special award, like extra time off, in exchange for delivering more or faster on my projects?

Sometimes people say to me, "Well, I have a boss, but we work as equal partners." If that's really true, then the answers to the questions why you need to manage your boss are clear: to reinforce and improve your partnership, to pour gasoline on the spark of your collaboration, to learn and grow together and as individuals. Maybe you can work together to improve productivity, quality, and innovation. Maybe you can challenge each other in unexpected ways. Maybe you can help each other reach greater heights of success than you ever would have on your own.

Then, of course, there are people who tell me, "This boss is different. He is so disengaged, so uninformed about my work, and so uninterested that he has nothing to offer me—and I need nothing from this boss." If that's truly the case, it doesn't mean you don't need a good working relationship with your boss. It just means this person is a boss in name only. Either you manage him, or you'll find yourself in a sink-or-swim situation.

3. What Do I Need to Talk About with This Boss?

Once you know why you need to manage this boss, you are well on your way to answering, "What do I need to talk *about* with this boss?" With every boss you need to talk about your work. When it comes to details, what you talk about with any boss should be determined by what you need to accomplish in the immediate future. For example, if you want help clarifying short-term priorities, then walk through your to-do list with that boss. If you want help improving your overall productivity, then talk about the number of items on your to-do list each day and ask for more assignments. Try to anticipate potential problems and talk about how to avoid them; identify problems and talk about how to solve them while they are still small.

Do you need to push, push, push or even trick your boss into talking about deadlines, schedules, time budgets, or whatever else is on your plate right now? Sometimes the answer is yes. With every boss, keep asking yourself, "What do I need to talk about *today*?"

4. How Should I Talk with This Boss?

Since every boss is different, you should communicate with each of them differently too. Some bosses respond best if you take an even-measured tone and stick to the facts—what I call the "auditor style." Some bosses respond best if you pepper them with leading questions—the "cross-examining-attorney style." Some bosses respond best to effusive enthusiasm; some, to worry, fear, and urgency. If you pay attention, you'll see that different bosses are more or less responsive to different manners and means of communication. It only makes sense to talk to bosses in their style—or at least to take into account their style. Some bosses are more challenging to communicate with than others.

An engineer on a design team told me about his boss—I'll call him Adam—who seemed unwilling to provide concrete timelines for work assignments. If this engineer or his coworkers asked about a deadline, schedule, or time budget, Adam always answered in roughly the same way. "If you asked him, 'What is the deadline?' Adam would just say, 'As soon as you can get it done.' If you asked him, 'Is there a schedule for this project?' he would just respond, 'We are going to get it done as soon as we can get it done.' If you asked him, 'How much time should we spend on this particular task?' Adam would just answer, 'Get it done as soon as you can get it done.' It was incredibly frustrating," the engineer confessed. But this frustrating situation led the engineers on his team to a clever "boss-managing" solution.

The engineer continued: "We all learned to pepper Adam with hypothetical time frames: 'Would a deadline of March 15 work?' and Adam would say, 'As soon as we can.' So we'd try again: 'Would April 15 work?' and Adam would say, 'As soon as we can.' We'd counter, 'May 15?' Finally, Adam would respond, 'Well, no. May 15 would be too late.' Ah ha! Now we were getting somewhere. We'd probe some more: 'What about May 1?' That's how we'd get a real deadline from him. Then we'd do the same thing with schedules and time budgets."

5. Where Should I Talk with This Boss?

Whether it's your boss's office or some other obvious place to meet, it's best to choose a place that is convenient for that boss—then make a habit of meeting there every time. That space will become the physical scene in which your management relationship with that boss will develop.

If you work in the same location with your boss, the best place to meet might be on some neutral ground. Is there a conference room or a cafeteria that might work? Where you meet for one-on-ones with each boss may also be determined in large part by the constraints of your work and your workplace. If you work in an environment where private spaces are not easily available, a quiet hallway, a stairwell, a walk to the lunchroom, or the organization's grounds will do as well. Finally, if you or your boss work in a remote location, you should rely primarily on a rigorous protocol of telephone calls and e-mails. (See Chapter Three.)

Wherever you get in the habit of meeting, just make sure you bring along a pad and pen so that you can write down and record everything.

6. When Should I Talk with This Boss?

When you are considering what days and times to meet with each boss, you are often limited by that boss's schedule and your own. The time at which you meet may be dictated completely by logistics. For example, if you work a different shift from that boss's, you may need to come in a little early or stay a little later to meet with her. It may be that the best time to meet is determined by that boss's moods, or by your own. Perhaps you have a boss who gets a slow start in the morning (or maybe you get a slow start), and so you decide it's best to meet with that boss just before lunch instead of first thing in the morning. Every one of your bosses will be different and will therefore require a different level of time commitment.

Although your bosses are all different, you probably need to talk to each one of them about your work more often than you do now. Err on the side of meeting more often than you think necessary with each boss, especially if your job is new or if you are working on a new task or project with this boss.

○ ○

Continue asking and answering these six questions about every single boss, and stay tuned to that boss as each of you grows and develops. Keep in mind that the answers to these questions are going to change with time. Your goal is to customize your work with each boss to establish well-functioning relationships with every one of them. You want every boss to look at you as the go-to employee on the most important tasks, responsibilities, and projects.

LEARN TO NEGOTIATE YOUR BOSSES' CONFLICTING PRIORITIES

Building a great one-on-one management dialogue with every boss is a lot easier to accomplish in a workplace with stable and clear reporting relationships and direct lines of accountability. But as we all know, in the real world such workplaces are rare. Some level of chaos is much more common. In the real world, you will encounter many complications that make it nearly impossible to maintain an airtight link between your actions and the accountability process you establish with each boss.

Every day I hear stories from employees who struggle to maintain stability and clarity in reporting relationships and lines of accountability. "There are just so many disruptions in that process," said a senior production supervisor in a multimedia entertainment behemoth. After years of interviews with her, I have come to refer to her as "the Major," since prior to working at the multimedia company she served for many years in the U.S. Army—an organization with a very tight chain of command.

"I learned in the army from necessity that you have to answer to anyone with rank," she told me. "You also know who you are reporting to at any given time. You know who is in command. But you have to keep everybody happy: it's one army. We all have the same mission. We try to help each other out. So you really answer to every soldier." She explained that in this orderly organization, although she received competing requests, rank and mission offered clear principles for sorting out priorities. "If Sergeant Smith asks me to do a task, I could say, 'I'm working on this other task for General Jones.' But then Sergeant Smith might respond, 'My thing is more mission-critical.' Then we might talk to General Jones together and the general would agree that mission-critical would almost always trump rank. The problem is that even if Sergeant Smith's task isn't mission-critical, he might still keep pushing me to take it on. He could say, 'Hey, c'mon

Major. I thought we were friends. Couldn't you do this for me as a favor when you have a chance?' And now I have this extra task to deal with."

How does the private sector differ, I asked her recently? "It's all the same stuff except that rank isn't always clear, and even if it is, there isn't an expectation that you will follow the chain of command. Plus, the mission-critical nature of the work isn't as clear. What takes priority? People don't necessarily agree on that."

The Major describes the conflicting lines of accountability in her organization: "For example, my immediate boss often goes around me and gives instructions to my production crew—often different instruction from what I've told them. It's very confusing for everyone. Who is my crew supposed to listen to? Me or my boss? Or [my boss's boss] might ask me to completely change my production schedule. Am I supposed to change it or should I check back with [my boss]? At the same time, I'm getting calls and e-mails from other people with their hands in the production. It's always different people, depending on the production. There might be real top dogs from another division of the company, or it might be on-air talent or a sponsor or an advertiser. I'm also getting calls and e-mails from content managers in the online properties, the different channels, for movies, from [the parent company], even for the magazines. I'm getting calls and e-mails from everyone trying to tell me what to do or what not to do or how to do my job."

The Major is legendary among her colleagues as being the coolest, calmest, most professional, and most successful production supervisor in the history of the company. How does she do that? Over the years, she has developed a way to deal

with these disruptions and conflicting priorities. So I asked her
to walk me through some work scenarios and explain how she
would respond to them:

What do you do . . .

. . . when your boss cuts you out of the chain of command by
giving assignments or instructions directly to your direct reports?

"Ask your boss, 'Did you mean to do that?' Then you have
to ask, 'Are you now going to manage this employee on this
assignment or instruction you've given, or do you want me to
do it? Do you want me to follow up with this employee? Would
you like to make the assignment or instruction clear to me so
that I can take it from here? Or are you going to take it from
here? And are you taking over this employee altogether? Or do
you want to share him with me?'"

. . . when your boss's boss end runs the chain of command and
gives you assignments directly?

"First, ask your boss's boss, 'Did you mean to do that?' Then
you have to ask, 'Do you want me to report to you on this assignment or to my boss? If I'm reporting to my boss on this,
maybe the three of us should discuss it together so we all have
the same understanding of the assignment? If I'm reporting directly to you on this, maybe the three of us should discuss how
it affects my available time?' Finally, make clear that your boss's
boss and your boss need to decide and make clear to you which
of your assignments take higher priority."

. . . when you have a problem with your immediate boss and
you want to end run the chain of command?

"Don't go over your boss's head unless you really need to.
First, decide if this is a big enough problem to threaten your
relationship with your immediate boss by going to his boss.
Ask yourself, 'Is the mission of your organization in danger

of failing? Will the consequences be serious? Is there a wrong being committed? Is it a pretty serious wrong?' Then, if you decide you have to go over your boss's head, your best bet is to go to a senior person you trust. Go with that senior person directly to your boss to try to resolve the problem. Hope for a resolution, or else it's going to be a dissolution—a dissolution of your relationship with that boss, and maybe with that job. You don't want to go over your boss's head lightly."

    ... *when dotted-line bosses or colleagues give you assignments?*

"First, figure out if you are the right and best person for the assignment. Second, determine the parameters of the assignment, such as how long it is going to take or what its requirements are. Third, decide if you have the time and if you want the assignment. Finally, ask yourself, 'Is it really up to me whether to take on this assignment? Do I need to check with my boss? Do I need to check with anyone else before I take it on?' Once you've figured all of this out, agree, with the person who assigned, on the parameters of the assignment and on how success is going to be measured."

    ... *when Ms. Big Shot calls out of the blue to give you an assignment, or tries to steal you away?*

"First, ask the big shot if they meant to assign the task to you. Remind them what your primary assignment is and that you mostly report to your boss. Second, figure out the parameters of the assignment and whether or not it is something you are capable of doing. Third, decide if the assignment will conflict with your ability to do your primary assignment for the boss you report directly to. If it does, then discuss this conflict with the big shot who is trying to borrow or steal you away. Finally, include the boss you directly report to in a conversation about this assignment—the earlier the better."

. . . when Mr. Peon Manager with a big ego calls out of the blue to give you an assignment, or tries to steal you away?

"First, feed this big ego a big snack. Heap deference, thanks, and praise on that big ego. Second, figure out if this assignment is something you need to deal with or whether you can brush it off. Usually, you can be honest and explain how busy you are on your other projects. You may get the boss you report to directly to weigh in for you. But you probably won't even need to. If you don't have time or a desire to take on this assignment, your best bet is to respond by recommending someone else. If it's someone calling you from out of the blue, they might as well call someone else out of the blue."

. . . when different managers impose conflicting rules or standards?

"Figure out right away if there is a source of authority on the rules or standards for the procedures, tasks, or responsibilities in question. If there is, then get a clear answer from that source and ideally a statement (perhaps from an instruction guide, e-mail from the source of authority, etc.): master it, follow it, and carry it around with you to offer as your answer whenever someone tells you otherwise. If there is no source of authority, or perhaps no right or wrong way of proceeding or doing the task or responsibility in question, then figure out what rules or standards each manager follows. If one of those managers asks you to follow a rule or standard that you know for a fact to be outright wrong or bad, then you'll need to try to teach that manager otherwise, or else try to avoid working for him or her, if that's an option."

. . . when Mr. Friend asks you to do extra work as a favor?

"You need to be able to distinguish between your real friends and people who are just friends out of convenience.

If this is a real friend, you might be willing to go out of your way for him or her. Before you do, perhaps you should ask, 'Is this something you really need me to do?' If it is not, then you might say, 'If you were really my friend, then you wouldn't ask me to do this, because I'm already way overworked.'"

Cultivate strong one-on-one management relationships with the best bosses. Keep your dance card full working for the best bosses. Then, take it one boss at a time, one day at a time.

CHAPTER FIVE

Make Sure You Understand What Is Expected of You

Your boss Chris just gave you what seems to be a great new assignment. Chris has heard good things about you and your work, and that's why he picked you for the project. This new, juicy project might even lead to new, ongoing responsibilities with potentially significant rewards for you—if you dazzle Chris with your work. You've never done anything quite like this but are eager and ready to learn. Chris gives you a large stack of documents and asks you "to read through it to get a feel for the material," admitting, "I'm not entirely sure what the final result should look like. What do you think it should look like?"

While you have a good discussion with Chris, in the end Chris doesn't spell out what concrete deliverables you are expected to turn in or any deadlines you are supposed to hit. Instead, Chris suggests that you talk with your colleague Pat, who completed a similar project recently. You and Chris agree that you will "figure it out" as you go along. After maybe a half hour discussing the few vague details of the assignment, Chris wraps up with one unmistakable point: "This project is a big priority." As you walk away with an armload of documents, Chris asks you to touch base in a few days to make sure things are going forward smoothly.

If you are on the receiving end of this assignment, then you have just been set up to fail on a very big opportunity. At the very least, you have been set up to accomplish a lot less than you are capable of. If you are very good, and really lucky, you might pull off a success on this project. Even if you get it right, however, you will feel as if you are in a sink-or-swim situation until you get the priorities of the project in order; a work plan in place to guide you; a schedule of concrete deliverables; deadlines for each task; and checklists to ensure the quality and completeness of your work.

By the time you've figured out the true parameters of the project, you might not be in a position to adequately finish it in time. There is probably a more concrete deadline than "this project is a big priority," and important specifications that you never even knew about—although you'll likely learn about them late into the project. You'll probably have to change course or make major changes to your work late in the game— and in a tremendous hurry. Chris will be thinking, "Why didn't you figure all this out earlier on in the project?" And you will certainly be thinking, "Gee, Chris, why didn't you tell me the real deadline and the important specifications for this project in the first place?"

Regardless of the outcome of the project, you will likely have enjoyed a suboptimal work experience; the end product will be less impressive than it could have been; Chris will not be as satisfied with your work (much less "dazzled"); and you will get less credit and reward than you could have. And it could be much worse: it could end in a costly disaster for you, for Chris, and for the company. Everybody involved will pay some share of the cost.

How could you possibly have handled this situation better to ensure the project's success, your success, and that of your boss's? The answer is by performing the first step in boss management: getting your boss to clarify expectations, including spelling out any specifications and deadlines that need to be met in order to secure the success of the project, task, or responsibility.

THE THREE KEY EXPECTATIONS YOU NEED TO GET FROM YOUR BOSS

No matter what type of work you do, from the outset of any assignment you need to make sure that you understand exactly what you are expected to do and exactly how you are expected to do it.

I am often surprised at how many people tell me, "I don't want to have a boss standing over my shoulder telling me what to do and how to do it all the time. They should just let me do my job." But then, in the next breath, many of these same people complain that their bosses fail to convey expectations clearly enough.

Perhaps you don't want a boss standing over your shoulder, but on the other hand, who do you blame when you discover after days or weeks or even months that you have been doing something wrong without even knowing it? Who do you blame when you realize you weren't told key details of your assignment? Who do you blame when you learn you weren't taught all the steps required in an important work process? You blame your boss.

While you may not want your boss standing over your shoulder telling you what to do and how to do it all the time, typically you don't have much to worry about: most managers don't have the time or inclination to do so. Sure, some managers don't hesitate to bark out step-by-step marching orders. As long as you can tolerate the bark and you can take notes quickly with a smile on your face, then there is a big upside to these managers: at least you know exactly what's expected of you. But the reality is that a huge number of managers do the opposite. They tell me, "I shouldn't have to tell my employees what to do and how to do it. They should know how to do their jobs already."

Often these bosses don't want to boss you around; they want you to feel a sense of "ownership" in your work. They like asking lots of questions and seeking input from you. They listen, make suggestions, and try to lead you to the right conclusions. They really want you to reach the right conclusions on your own. They often say, "I like to let employees learn from their own mistakes."

I think, what cruel bosses! Why wouldn't they want to help their employees avoid unnecessary mistakes? Why wouldn't they help you learn to do things really well by practicing doing things right? It is simply a fallacy that practicing wrong ways of doing things is a good way to learn how to do things right. If you have to reinvent the wheel every time you do a new task, responsibility, or project, then you will probably spend too much time developing bad habits from inadvertently learning and practicing bad techniques. Trial and error is a good way to solve a unique problem, but it is not a good way to learn an established best practice, task, or responsibility.

And it's certainly not the way to give you "ownership" of your work. After all, you are paid to do specific tasks within closely defined parameters. It's actually *not* up to you what you do at work and how you do it. You "own" your job only when you know what you are supposed to do and how you are supposed to do it—including what is *not* up to you, and exactly what *is*. Only when you understand exactly what is required of you and exactly where you have discretion to make decisions and take action are you truly empowered.

Real power in the workplace rarely comes in the form of being left alone to do whatever you think should be done however you think it should be done. Rather, power comes from having the responsibility to accomplish specific tasks and projects in certain ways at certain times delegated to you.

Most managers who adopt a "facilitative" approach to managing (helping you "figure things out on your own") rather than an explicitly "directive" approach (delegating tasks by giving clear directions and spelling out expectations) do so because it's much easier to sidestep the uncomfortable tension that comes from telling other people exactly what to do.

But you need clear marching orders. The real trick to gaining power through effective delegation is helping your bosses figure out the goals, guidelines, and timelines that are appropriate for each assignment. To do so, you need to maintain an ongoing dialogue with them about every assignment on your to-do list. This is the only way to ensure you are getting the three key elements essential to understanding what

is expected of you for every project, task, or responsibility assigned to you:

- Clear goals: Establish what the end product should look
  like. What deliverables are you responsible for completing?
- Detailed parameters: Learn the specifications and requirements for each individual project, task, or responsibility
  assigned to you. How do you need to do this task?
- Accurate deadlines: Determine when you are expected
  to complete the project. What is the schedule of deliverables for all the steps necessary to meet this goal?

Whenever you are expected to do a project or task, then
you must engage your boss in order to provide you these three
key elements. You must get him or her to spell out in vivid
detail exactly what you are expected to do. If you are expected
to do something in a particular way, then you need to talk
with your boss until he or she spells out in clear and specific
detail exactly what specifications you are expected to follow.
At the very least, you need to know the bare minimum requirements and the gold standard of performance; the cardinal rules
of conduct and the outer limits of your discretion. No matter
how self-sufficient, responsible, and hardworking you may be,
nobody can function successfully on a sustained basis without
at least some structure and boundaries.

WHAT TO DO IF YOUR BOSS DOESN'T PROVIDE CLEAR EXPECTATIONS

If you are working with a boss who has a hard time spelling
out expectations in clear, specific detail, then you might need

to help him or her out. As mentioned earlier, many bosses follow a "facilitative approach"; that is, they have been taught that it is better to ask employees questions to lead them to the right answers rather than be directive. Unfortunately, the three most common questions managers ask their employees are exactly the wrong questions:

- "How is everything going?"
- "Is everything on track?"
- "Are there any problems I should know about?"

These questions take you nowhere, because they are not specific enough. Indeed, the conversations between bosses and employees should be interactive dialogues. But they should never turn into guessing games. If your boss is going to try to manage you by asking questions, then help that boss ask really good questions.

The questions your manager should be asking and the questions you need to be answering in dialogue with your boss are:

- "Can you complete this assignment? What do you need from me in order to complete this assignment?" "What additional information, training, tools, materials, space, money, or people might I need? If I'll be lacking in any necessary resources, what workarounds might I consider? How much discretion do I have to try workarounds as I go?"

- "What is your plan for achieving this assignment? Have you set a schedule for meeting deadlines along the way? What date and time is the first reporting milestone? What initial steps will you follow? What will be the benchmarks for success at that milestone?"

- "Have you created a to-do list or checklist for each step of the project? How long will step one take? What guidelines are you following for step one? What about steps two, three, four, and so on?"

When *you* are able to answer these questions about an assignment, then you know you have clear expectations about the work that needs to be done. When you are able to talk through the answers with your boss, then you know for sure that you and your boss have the same expectations. If you and your boss both take clear notes while you talk through the answers, then you can both double-check that you're "on the same page."

If your boss isn't asking these questions of you, then you should be asking and answering the very same questions yourself—or asking your boss to help you think through the answers aloud. Listen carefully to your boss's input and take notes every step of the way. Use those written notes as a tool in your next conversation with your boss to further clarify expectations for your performance on this work and to make sure you are still on the same page.

Maintaining clear expectations is an ongoing process of clarifying and fine-tuning, working and talking, getting on the same page and staying on the same page.

MANAGING EXPECTATIONS IN THE MIDST OF CONSTANT CHANGE

People often say to me, "Even when I spend time talking with my boss about the work in advance, the problem is that things so often change. What we decided yesterday no longer holds today."

The classic example is the I.T. department of just about any organization. As one I.T. services manager in a scientific research company told me: "The nature of my job is keeping your computer working. That's always an emergency: If your computer isn't working, you can't work. But you never know in advance when a computer is going to break down. When out of nowhere your computer stops working, you become my number one priority, regardless of what my boss and her team may have discussed last night about what my priorities were going to be for today. Our work load is heavy, and the flow is not steady. So we have to constantly triage the work coming in to assess it for priority level against the existing workload."

He continued: "There are usually two different points during the day where I touch base with my boss: In the morning, we review the list of work orders and decide who is going to do what; and at the end of the day on our way out the door we look at what's happened during the day and what the next day is probably going to look like. But when those calls come during the day or at night, I can quickly reshuffle the priorities. I always have to ask myself, 'What's the priority for *me* at the moment?'"

Maybe once in a while (or often, depending on your job or the industry in which you work) your boss says to you: "Yesterday I said the most important things were A, B, and C. Well, from now on, they don't matter. Sorry about all that work we started doing on them. Now the most important things are X, Y, and Z." Is that somehow evidence that your boss didn't really know what the heck was going on yesterday? Maybe so. But probably not. The reality of today's workplace is constant change. When priorities change, expectations change. That's why it's even more critical for you to be engaging in an ongoing management conversation with your boss. Every time a shift or change requires a significant adjustment or course correction in priorities and expectations, you need to make sure you ask your boss the following questions:

- What has shifted and changed, and what adjustments and course corrections do I need to make?
- How do I need to change or adjust my resource plan?
- How do I need to reprioritize my to-do list of concrete actions?
- Has the checklist to ensure quality control for every concrete action changed as a result of this shift in priorities?
- What priorities should I be focused on as of right now?

RETAINING YOUR CREATIVITY WHILE CLARIFYING EXPECTATIONS AND DEFINING BOUNDARIES

Most people want to be free to make some decisions at work. You don't want to operate like a soldier all day. In fact, you may even be expected to be a little bit creative in your job, which requires you to take some risks and make a few mistakes—and you like it that way. How then is it possible to get clear expectations and directives from your boss, especially if your whole job is about creating something new and different?

The more creative you want to be in your work, the more critical it is for you to be 100 percent clear about what is expected of you and, in particular, what is and what is not within your discretion. You need to understand exactly the parameters within which you are expected to operate. If you are given no guidelines or goals, you still want to clearly define some boundaries; otherwise, you may find yourself completely adrift. At the very least you want to find out whether there is a deadline. Or will you be allowed to brainstorm ad infinitum? How will you know when you are "done"? How will you recognize a finished product or result? If you are going to be free to take risks and make mistakes, then you need to get your boss to define parameters in order to create a space in which risk-taking and mistakes are truly safe for you in the context of this job.

Beware. Sometimes when you are given a "creative" assignment, what's really going on is that your boss just doesn't yet have a clear goal for the project in mind. He doesn't know exactly what he is looking for yet, so he asks you to "take a crack at it" so that he can look at it and "take it from there." This is nothing more than your boss using you to work out the early stages of his or her creative process. But if you and the boss have not talked through that process in advance and you do not understand exactly what your role in the assignment is, this can turn into a frustrating experience for both of you. You may end up working hard on the project, only to have him send it back to the drawing board over and over, or take over entirely to rework it himself. You then feel that the manager has hijacked the project and that your work and efforts have been for nothing. Even if the goals of an assignment are uncertain, it is still critical that you learn what role the boss wants you to play in it, and understand exactly what is expected of you.

WHEN YOUR BOSS IS NOT THE EXPERT

Oftentimes bosses oversee employees who have particular expertise that they may not share. If you are an expert and your boss doesn't have the knowledge or experience of doing your job, how do you get any guidance from him or her? Teach. Your boss doesn't have to become an expert on the work you are doing. But you do have to teach your boss enough to understand what you are doing.

It's okay that your boss doesn't know or understand everything you may be doing. But it's not okay for your boss to remain totally in the dark. When trying to get your boss to spell out expectations, focus on outcomes and ask lots of questions: "Exactly what is it you want me to accomplish? What do you want to be holding in your hands in the end? What is the effect you are looking for?" Help your boss do the homework so that she can ask you probing questions during your management conversations and make sure you are on the right track to meeting her expectations. Keep her informed and focused on outcomes: "This is where we are now. This is how long it took to get here. This is what I am going to do next. This is why. This is how long it should take. This is what we should have at the end of this stage." Document the basics of these conversations.

While your boss may never become an expert, over time he will get to know your work better and better, and should get better and better at helping you clarify expectations for your performance.

GET INTO THE RHYTHM OF YOUR WORK

Getting your boss to clarify expectations and spell out specifications and deadlines to secure the success of your projects, tasks, or responsibilities is your first priority when it comes to managing your boss. Besides getting clear expectations from your manager, however, you'll need to get into the rhythm of your work to fully stay on top of changing priorities and expectations.

I've spent a lot of time observing and talking with people who work in complex, rapidly changing, pressure-filled environments—workplaces in constant motion, where everyone is in a hurry and multitasks, and everyone must work with and depend on one another. If you are employed in one of these workplaces, you may not be sure what matters most at every moment of the day, what you are supposed to be focused on, or what your priority should be—and you may not have access to your boss to get clarification on these rapidly shifting priorities.

"The key to succeeding in any work situation is getting into the rhythm of the set patterns," said one wise sage of the workplace, who over the years has worked in five pressure-filled workplaces—as an army medic, EMT in a civilian ambulance, emergency room nurse, intensive care nurse, and after a total career change, as a restaurant entrepreneur.

The sage continues: "I know some managers are very good at organizing their people so that most of their employees are into the rhythm. They keep everyone in sync with the changing priorities. They have a sheet of music for everyone to play off, a checklist for everyone—from the top to the bottom job— to help everyone stay in tune with the rhythm of the place.

"My advice is, wherever you work, whether your manager is good at helping you or not, pay attention to the rhythm of work and learn your part of the music by heart, so you always know exactly what you are supposed to be doing at any point depending on where you are in the rhythm. . . . The unexpected is an expected part of the rhythm. I learned in the army, when the unexpected happens, that's when you need most for the training to kick in."

What does that really mean? It means you should know the standard operating procedures for just about every situation in your job. "When things are most unpredictable is when you need the standard operating procedures the most," he argues. If you work in a place without clear rules of engagement, without standard operating procedures for the expected or the unexpected, "you need to come up with your own standard operating procedures," he concludes. "Make your own checklists. . . . Write your own sheet of music, and play it as best you can every day. If you are the only one who can get into the rhythm, then you'll be 'the one.' You'll be walking through the hail of fire unscathed, doing your own thing very well, helping everyone else out. That's how you become a peer leader."

CHAPTER SIX

Assess and Plan
for the Resources
You Need

E very assignment, task, or responsibility requires its own set of resources. Without the necessary resources—skills, tools, materials, and people support—it is much more difficult to accomplish your job, whatever it may be. Unfortunately, sometimes you might not have the proper resources to do the tasks assigned to you, and you might not even realize it—until it's too late. If that's the case, you may be trying to push a boulder uphill using brute force, not knowing that a pulley is available to do the job more easily. And the boulder will most likely keep rolling back down. If you don't even know what resources you lack, then you are not being set up for success.

As soon as your boss assigns you a new project, task, or responsibility, you need to ask two questions: Do I have the basic ability (experience, wisdom, creativity, attitude, authority, and influence) to do this task? And, Do I have enough time? The answers to these two questions will allow you to figure out your "productive capacity." Your productive capacity is the most basic resource you have to rely on to get just about anything done.

Everything else—tools, space, materials, other people's support and time—is a variable in the *resource planning* you must do for every project. And the person who ought to help you figure out your resource plan for a project is your boss. If your boss is not volunteering that assistance when he or she assigns the project, then it's your responsibility to bring it up and get the information you need at your next one-on-one management conversation.

WHAT IS RESOURCE PLANNING?

"Every resource plan begins with a complete inventory of primary resources needed to get a job done," says Meredith, the long-serving resource-planning chief of a giant multinational energy-services conglomerate. "That means work space, supplies, infrastructure, utilities, materials, equipment, transportation, information, plus operation and maintenance. That means people, talent, training, effort, communication and cooperation, and most important, time. No matter how big or small your project, there are major strategic advantages you can gain from good resource planning: productivity, quality, and a better work experience."

You already do resource planning in your everyday life—from stocking toilet paper to making sure the gas tank in your car is full—and when you don't, you probably run into trouble and regret your lack of planning.

"Resource planning is invisible if everything is going right," Meredith explains. Without resource planning, no complex endeavor will get off the ground. With bad resource planning, any complex endeavor will sputter and then grind to a halt. But the same is true with more straightforward endeavors too—it's just less obvious.

"There is nothing like finding out, after you have completed a big job, that there was a resource available that could have helped you do it a lot faster or a lot better or with a lot less effort. You think, 'If only I had known about that resource!' Or have you ever gotten deep into a job and realized that you absolutely need some resource, only to discover that the resource is unavailable? If that's the case, it is more likely that your job outcome will meet lower standards than you have promised or than is expected from you. Even if the resource is available, your work will incur an interruption while you obtain the missing resource."

To do resource planning right, you need to follow three basic steps—and involve your boss in every one of them in order to make sure you get the resources you need to succeed in your job:

Step One: Inventory the primary resources you will need to accomplish the task assigned to you. Make sure you know what resources you'll need to complete your project.

Step Two: Research the "supply chain." Figure out whether the needed resource is available and, if so, from what source. What is the process, cost, and turnaround time for obtaining that resource?

Step Three: Identify possible workarounds. If you need resources that are unavailable, you must prepare a "plan B" to complete the job by working around the lack of those resources.

If your boss doesn't have this information, can he or she at least help you figure out who might?

STEP ONE: INVENTORY THE PRIMARY RESOURCES YOU WILL NEED TO ACCOMPLISH YOUR TASK

The first step in involving your boss in resource planning is asking, "What are the primary resources I need to accomplish the project or task you've assigned to me?" This is a simple habit you can build into your ongoing management conversations. You need to talk through the resources you will need with your boss. You need his or her guidance and direction. You might even need your boss's direct help or intervention.

I've learned from training many people that the following list covers just about any potential resources you might need to accomplish your project—no matter what that project is. You can use this list as a tool to help you in your discussions with your boss. Ask whether you need, or need to adjust, any of the following resources:

Work space

Supplies

Materials

Equipment

Transportation

Information

Operation

Maintenance

People

Talent

Training

Communication

Cooperation

For every assignment, task, responsibility, and project, some resource categories on this list will not be relevant. Maybe some of the resource categories will be irrelevant to most of your work. If so, take a moment to think of the resources that are required to get your work done and create a list that you can use in your one-on-one management dialogues.

Whether you use the list above or one of your own, the one resource that you will always need is time. To create a comprehensive resource plan for any task, responsibility, or project assigned to you, always build in enough turnaround time for every resource acquisition. This means allowing enough time to prepare your resource request, have it be processed, and then receive the resource. Creating this timeline is critical to good resource planning, and to do it accurately you'll need to do what I call "supply chain research."

STEP TWO: RESEARCH THE "SUPPLY CHAIN"

Realizing you need a particular resource to complete a job is one thing. And it is no small thing, as discussed above. But the real trick is getting your hands on the resources you need. Some resources are a whole lot easier to come by than others. Once you've figured out with your boss what resources you need in order to complete your project, you need to find out whether the resources are available and, if they are, from what source and at what cost. What is the process for getting these resources? Talk through every aspect of the "supply chain" for your resources with your boss: What sources should you check to find out whether a resource is available? What process should you follow to get the resource? What turnaround time should you expect? What should you do in the event you run into roadblocks?

Oftentimes you'll find you need resources that have to be purchased. Make sure you discuss with your boss any resource you may need up front that you or your department will have to buy. Is there a budget for that?

"I find new professionals coming to our company from the private sector have to get used to the fact that we have very tight budgeting and a very strict approval process for spending any discretionary funds," said a senior executive in a large international charitable nonprofit organization, which I've worked with over the years. "No matter where you work, you would be smart to learn how the budgeting is done. How do you tap the discretionary budgets? Who can approve spending? For what amounts and what kinds of purchases?"

The ability to buy stuff is important. If you need to go shopping for the resources necessary to do your job, then the path to obtaining those things will be clear and straightforward if you have a budget and a purchase process.

"Buying a test tube is easy. What is much more difficult and far more common is all the various things I need to get from people, both internally and externally," explains a senior science program manager in a medical research institute, where I have spent weeks consulting and training. "So often what I need is a piece of information, ten words, or maybe a document. Or maybe I need something like an approval from someone in another department. Maybe I need someone in I.T. to set up a computer or install some software. Or maybe I need an external vendor, like a travel agency, to arrange a trip for me. These are all resources I need, but none of them are straight-forward purchases. What I really need in each of these cases is the informal cooperation and assistance of another person, usually a person who does not work for me exactly, but I need to depend on this person to provide a service for me."

Often what you need then to do your job will be resources that don't cost money exactly but instead require the infor-mal cooperation and assistance of another person, internal and external to your department or division. You may need something from a person with whom the precise nature of your working relationship is not entirely clear.

In your one-on-one management dialogues, talk with your boss to anticipate together what cooperation and assistance you might need from other colleagues—internal and exter-nal—to get a project or task completed. Talk through the fol-lowing questions together: Exactly whom should you ask for what, and when and how? What is the precise nature of your working relationship with each person on whom you may need to rely? What level of cooperation and assistance is appropriate and reasonable to request? In each case, could you turn to more than one person for cooperation and assistance? What should you do if you are having trouble getting cooperation and as-sistance from someone?

You should also ask your boss for his or her help in iden-tifying the people in the organization who can help you get the resources you need—and then further help in developing strong relationships with them.

"The best thing you can do over time is develop good work-ing relationships with key people in key areas," says the savvy science program manager. "These become your *go-to people*.

These are people you know you can rely on. They are responsive. They are effective. They get things done. These are people who know that you do your part, too. You help them do their job well when they are working with you. You learn to work well together. You develop a relationship with a go-to person in another area by becoming the go-to person in *your* area."

According to several of this manager's colleagues, that's exactly how she conducts herself in the medical research institute. "She bends over backward to do things for other people, not just on her program, but all over [the institute]," says one of her colleagues. "I'd say I owe her plenty of favors. Even if I didn't owe her a single favor, I'd go way out of my way to do things for her, just because of how she is, her manner, her attitude. She carries a lot of weight with people just because she is so no-nonsense, such a doer, such a strong corporate citizen. She earns respect just by the way she conducts herself. She has everybody's deep personal respect. She has that incredible reputation, and that gives her a lot of interpersonal power with everyone."

And yet, this colleague insists, there is nothing "personal" about the power and respect she carries: "She is all business. It's not loyalty that grows from a personal connection. It's a loyalty that grows from how she does business."

Start by building those important interpersonal connections with colleagues—internally and externally—by consistently conducting yourself as a strong corporate citizen, a doer, and a no-nonsense professional. Ask yourself: How do I conduct myself at work? How do I do business with my colleagues? What is my attitude? What kind of reputation do I have? Keep asking yourself these questions every step of the way and be rigorously honest with yourself.

What if you are not a go-to person for your area yet?

Well, sometimes you have to bake cookies. A much less experienced science program manager in the same research institute says: "I am new around here. I haven't had time to build a reputation and develop go-to people from years of working together. But I still have to rely on people throughout the institute. So I bake a lot of cookies. I've broken down barriers and opened up doors and built strong working relationships with people all over the institute in a very short period of time; actually, one plate of cookies at a time."

And sometimes you need your boss to weigh in for you. Resource planning should be an ongoing part of your management dialogues with your boss, but you should especially talk with your boss whenever you run into a roadblock in this area.

The science program manager offers the following advice for when to ask your boss to intervene on your behalf: "There are two instances when your boss should intervene: One is when you are just not getting a response from someone, because they don't know who you are or you don't have a big enough title. Second, when the person you need to get some information or a document from might be a senior executive or someone who is intimidating to deal with, or you don't want to push too hard because he or she is powerful or important."

STEP THREE: IDENTIFY POSSIBLE WORKAROUNDS

What if you simply cannot get your hands on the resources you need to do your job? Do you throw your hands up in frustration and declare, "There's nothing I can do!" Absolutely not. Declaring forfeit is the great mantra of the powerless. Don't say it. Don't think it.

If you don't have access to the resources you need to do your job, then you have to work around that resource gap and do the job as best you can without it. You need a plan B. Any successful person with significant work experience is quite familiar with the "workaround."

Let me give you an example from a longtime producer at a small-venue theater: "The show must go on! Because of the scale of our productions, we don't have formal understudies, so we try to have informal understudies in the cast for every show. Often that doesn't happen. So if one cast member has to play a second part at the last minute and isn't prepared, they might have to have the script in hand for the second part and read the lines. If the actor needs to play two characters who appear in a number of scenes together, we have to have another cast member play a role that doesn't make sense for that person, like a young woman needs to also play the part of an old man. Sometimes we'll have a non–cast member, a nonactor, just stand in with a script in hand—actually filling in the part with a stand-in reader rather than an actor. This is not ideal, but sometimes we have to do it. The show must go on."

These are real but of course drastic workarounds! Any time you might have to do a workaround, you should plan to talk it through with your boss and get his or her guidance and direction in planning your workaround. Whenever possible, it makes sense to talk about potential workarounds well in advance, in the earliest stages of resource planning, and then continue the conversation every step of the way. As you anticipate necessary resources, as you discuss what sources to try and how to get what you need, you should also consider—and talk about—what to do if despite your best efforts you are still not able to get the resources you need.

Resource workarounds almost always follow four steps, progressively:

1. Seek a substitute source for your resource. If a book you need to complete a research report isn't available at your local libraries or bookstores, then you might look for it in another store further away or through online retailers. Perhaps the price point and turnaround time drive you to choose yet another source, such as used bookstores or online sellers of used books.

2. Seek a substitute resource. In the theater example above, in the absence of the original cast member, the producer relies on an understudy to play the role. If there are no understudies, cast members stand in.

3. Innovate or come up with a method of completing the task that doesn't involve the resource you originally felt you needed. One of my favorite examples of innovation bred by a resource gap was told to me by a onetime short-order cook (now turned entrepreneur), who worked for some time in a busy diner:

   "We were selling a lot of fried food. Most of it we were cooking in a fry-o-later, obviously," he shared with me one day. "But we had this ancient fry-o-later, which had a lot of problems. The owner was too cheap to replace it. So about half the time the fry-o-later was down. Try doing a busy lunch at this place without fries and onion rings and cheese sticks and chicken tenders. That's how I invented griddle-fry. I used the griddle with a layer of oil, and I'd fry everything up on the griddle. When the fry-o-later was working, people would order griddle-fries, griddle-onion-rings, griddle-cheese-sticks, griddle-chicken-tenders. It turns out, everything tastes better when it's made on a griddle."

Necessity is the mother of invention. If you don't have the resources to do the job properly, you might have to devise a way to do the job differently. Maybe that different way of doing the job will be delicious.

4. Sometimes, in the face of a fundamental resource gap, there is nothing you can do but try harder. Your only choice might be to employ much greater time and energy to make up for the missing resource. Don't underestimate the value of this one, because so often it is the only workaround available: Try harder!

THE IMPORTANCE OF KEEPING YOUR BOSS INVOLVED

Too many bosses will leave you to your own devices to figure out how to get the resources you need to get your projects, tasks, or responsibilities done. Perhaps of all the boss-management tools, ensuring that you get the help you need from your boss is the most important. It's especially important to continue getting the attention of your manager if you either cannot secure the resources you need on your own, or must come up with a workaround or plan B.

If your boss is not volunteering to help you, then inform him or her every step of the way on your decision making, so that if you have to make a call on your own—whether it is securing a resource that is not readily available, enlisting the cooperation of someone outside your department, or coming up with a plan B—there will be no surprises. The more you talk about your decisions up front, the fewer tough conversations you'll have with your boss down the road.

CHAPTER SEVEN

Track Your Own Performance Every Step of the Way

Have you ever had a boss about whom you could say, "This boss knows exactly who I am and what I am doing, and she really, really cares"? This is a boss who knows what you've worked on in the past, what you are working on now, and what you are going to be working on next. Who constantly takes thorough, organized, accurate notes, and encourages you to do the same. Who is all over the details, telling you, through her actions, that you and the work you do are important.

What about the opposite end of the spectrum? Have you had a boss who didn't keep track of your day-to-day performance? This is the boss who never seems to know what you are doing or why you are doing it. Who often doesn't even know your whereabouts. Who is out of the loop. Who tells you, through his actions, that neither you nor your work is all that important.

No matter which of these bosses you have, it is up to you to make sure that *you* are all over the details when it comes to keeping track of your own performance. Employees who track their own day-to-day performance closely have no surprises when the time comes for midyear and annual reviews. Employees who are all over the details are powerful because bosses and coworkers consider them to be self-starting high-performers.

These employees have written records going back months or years that reflect their assignments and performance of tasks, responsibilities, and projects. They always work from a plan and regularly update their goals and timelines, routinely checking things off a to-do list and taking notes every step of the way. One of their mantras is, "Let me write that down." They take thorough, organized, accurate notes and then refer to those notes in subsequent conversations with their boss. In fact, they keep such close track of things in writing that their manager often relies more on their written records than the manager's own system.

By contrast, employees who do *not* keep close track of their own day-to-day performance are likely to have trouble recalling what tasks, responsibilities, and projects they did yesterday, much less those they accomplished weeks and months ago. They do not work from a plan, have clearly articulated goals and timelines, or make good use of a schedule or a to-do list; instead, they are likely to work from various piles on their desk and floor. They rarely take notes, and when they do, they are likely to make scrawls that are difficult to discern later on— and these "notes" usually end up in one of the piles. These employees often call or e-mail or walk back to the boss to ask for clarification, even on routine assignments; some assignments end up slipping through the cracks because they have quite simply been forgotten. Conversations with these employees often require untangling differing recollections about what has been said in the past. When it comes to midyear and end-of-year reviews—not to mention the evaluation of work product on an ongoing basis—these employees sometimes encounter unwelcome surprises. Such employees have little power because bosses and coworkers consider them to be low, or at most mediocre, performers.

Which type of employee are you? Are you all over the details of your performance? Or are you totally out of your own loop? My guess is that, like most people, you find yourself somewhere in the middle.

Here's what most people do when tracking their own performance: they keep a record of things that are *easy* to track. If you already keep a schedule or punch a clock, it is easy to keep track of the hours you have worked. If you already keep an organized set of folders with e-mails you've sent and received, it is easy to track your correspondence. Maybe certain numbers related to your work are generated by a computer system. For example, if you are a salesperson, you might have bottom-line numbers of sales calls made, conversations completed, follow-up materials sent, contracts booked, dollars received, and monthly or weekly sales reported. If you work at a help desk, you probably have numbers on the help calls received, help tickets logged, and help tickets cleared. And so on.

But even when much of what they do is tracked electronically, most people do not keep track of their own day-to-day performance in writing. And few managers keep close track of employee performance in writing, either. Most bosses track employee performance only incidentally: when they happen to observe the employee working; when they are presented with the employee's work product; and when there is a big win or a notable problem. In fact, most bosses rarely document employee performance unless they are required to do so, thus leaving no written track record other than those bottom-line electronic reports. The problem is that the numbers often tell very little about the day-to-day actions that you can control.

THE POWER OF TRACKING YOUR PERFORMANCE IN WRITING

The more closely you track your own performance, the more power you will have to

- Seek guidance, direction, on-the-job training, and coaching

- Identify resource needs and justify requests

- Evaluate your performance against the expectations you agree on with your boss every step of the way

- Help your boss keep track of your successes; anticipate problems; and get your boss's help in solving small problems as they occur

- Plan your work and adjust your plans on an ongoing basis

- Keep setting ambitious but meaningful goals and deadlines

- Gain more and more responsibility

- Give a regular, accurate report of your performance to your boss

- Help your boss link your high performance to increased rewards

Once you start to be "all over the details," you will gain respect and power in your working relationships with every boss and every coworker. Armed with written tracking records, you will be in a position to take on more and more responsibility, make better judgment calls, and take action more effectively in everything you do. You'll be able to clarify expectations for yourself and help your boss set you up for success. You will also radically accelerate your productivity and reduce your error rates, even as you take on more and more important work. If things go wrong, you'll be able to see exactly where and when and how they went wrong, and demonstrate that you were doing your best every step of the way. When it's time to seek extra rewards for above-and-beyond performance, you will have a detailed written record to help you make your case and secure more generous rewards.

The greater your reputation for being all over the details, the more credible you will be. This doesn't mean you pretend to know things that you don't. Indeed, having a reputation for being thorough, organized, responsible, and knowledgeable gives you a lot of latitude to admit when you don't know something. Nobody will think you are dumb because you are asking questions or deliberating checking the facts.

Likewise, the greater your reputation for keeping track of things and reporting regularly, candidly, and fully on your work—good, bad, and average—the more trust you will build with each of your bosses. A boss will be much more likely to trust you and rely on your interpretations of events when you have proven yourself reliable and trustworthy. If the boss has confidence that you are double-checking and triple-checking your details, keeping track of them in writing, and reporting thoroughly and honestly, then the boss won't need to duplicate that effort by scrutinizing every detail of your work.

That point was brought home to me by an inventory manager who manages supervisors in an auto parts company: "I make it a point to spot-check every supervisor's orders database. Which supervisors don't get much spot-checking? If I have a supervisor who I know is meticulous, then I don't need to spot-check very often. I have one supervisor who prints out the orders placed and orders received and the receiving schedule every day. If there is even a hair out of place, she won't go home without getting it resolved. If something doesn't get resolved, I hear about it from her immediately. Why would I spot-check that supervisor? I don't need to do that with her.

"But I do spot-check some of the supervisors every day, especially those who try to sweep problems under the rug. There is always something I can find, and I make sure to let those supervisors know that I noticed that something. I need to make sure they think I'm keeping track even more than I really am, that I might be looking over their shoulder at any given moment."

If you want to be considered meticulous and be trusted by your boss, then you need a tracking system to document your own performance on a daily basis. Tracking your own performance in writing will add much clarity to your management relationship. Simply talking about expectations and performance is not enough. Writing down the details allows you to confirm with each boss, every step of the way: "I want to make sure I understand. This is what I'm writing down. Please take a look. Is this your understanding, too?"

Tracking in writing is a powerful way to create in both you and your boss a psychological commitment to the expectations that you have agreed on together. You and your boss are also sharing the experience of creating a written record, which can be referred to later so you won't have to wrestle with competing recollections. Knowing that every expectation is included in a written record creates a lot of pressure on you to live up to the commitments you make. But it also puts important pressure on your boss to make sure that each and every time you are given an assignment, the expectations are spelled out clearly and the performance being tracked in writing consists of concrete actions within your control, not simply a bunch of numbers that are disconnected from the day-to-day expectations spelled out for your performance.

Beyond all that, your written records help you to evaluate for yourself, and make the case to your boss, whether you deserve any special rewards or detriments based on your performance. Those written records become even more important in the event of a formal dispute because you will have a much easier time confirming, for yourself and your boss, whether you are being treated fairly in relation to your performance. That documentation will provide a paper trail to support your version of the facts.

Tracking is also the key to taking charge of your own ongoing performance improvement. The constant self-evaluation that comes from tracking in writing your boss's feedback will help you help your boss revise and adjust your marching orders. If your boss says, "You did a great job on A, B, and C. But on D, you failed fully to complete items D3, D4, and D5 on the to-do list," you will know that your next goal is to focus on D3, D4, and D5. You need to talk through D3, D4, and D5 in detail with your boss right then, noting every detail about what you will need to accomplish to complete those items. In fact, this would be a good time to make a step-by-step checklist for yourself for D3, D4, and D5, which you will be able to use as a guide for completing and quality-checking your work. Later, you can use that same tool as a point of reference to guide your discussion with the boss when the two of you review your performance on D3, D4, and D5.

TRACK YOUR PERFORMANCE BY MONITORING YOUR OWN CONCRETE ACTIONS

If your boss is like most managers, she probably monitors mostly the elements of your performance that are easy to notice, such as your hours in the office or the daily reports and weekly spreadsheets she automatically receives. But knowing exactly when you come and go or having business data in hand doesn't really reflect what you are actually *doing* during those hours at work. Tracking your real, concrete actions tells much more about your performance, but it does take a lot more effort. If your boss isn't going to put in that effort on her own, then you have to help. And even if she does monitor your concrete actions, you also need to monitor them yourself.

"Once you begin tracking your own performance in writing," a very smart boss-manager told me, "you become much more aware of your strengths and weaknesses. When it's a question of what you have actually done today, it gets a lot harder to fool yourself. When you can see in black and white exactly what you are doing and how it's going, everything gets really clear. Between us, either my boss or I will see much sooner if something isn't going quite right, and we can make some changes right then and there. Before we used the written tracking, we had a lot more problems that stayed undetected for way too long. There were a lot more surprises."

An employee I'll call Jake learned that lesson the hard way. Jake was an ambitious, hardworking new employee in the clinical testing laboratory of a medical research company. His job was to welcome the test subjects when they arrived and to facilitate the intake process, which was similar—yet different in important ways—to the process he had followed in a previous job. The problem began on his first day, when Jake mistakenly assumed that certain steps that seemed similar to the process he had followed at his old job should be done the same way at the new job. Jake told his boss, who was teaching him the intake process, that he understood how to complete these steps—but he was wrong.

"When it comes to clinical testing, consistency is very important, even regarding administrative details such as the way intake forms are completed," Jake said. "If you don't do certain things correctly, the test subject can't be counted in the data. The steps I was following were inconsistent with the intake process they had been using, so my test subjects got thrown out of the data.

"I was touching base with my boss regularly, telling her everything was going just great," Jake continued. "But three weeks later, when she sat down to quality-check my paperwork, she saw the mistakes I was making. That was an awful feeling. Weeks of work wasted." He concluded the story with this: "I really learned my lesson and so did my boss. You can't assume that everything is going well unless you are really drilling down into the details and looking closely at your work with your boss. If I had come to her earlier and asked her to take a close look at the paperwork to make sure I was doing it right, I would have gotten on the right track the very next day." Wasn't it the boss's responsibility to more closely monitor Jake's performance, to check the work carefully to make sure it was being done right? Says Jake, "Maybe so. But we both paid the price. We both looked bad. It cost us both plenty of aggravation."

If your boss isn't keeping close enough track of your performance, then you need to help him monitor your performance. Here are five ways to do that:

Provide drafts or samples of your work in progress on a regular basis. Jake's experience makes the importance of this method clear. If you want to make sure the work you are doing meets your boss's requirements, don't wait until a routine review of the work comes along; by then you might discover you've been doing a task the wrong way for quite some time. Even if you have a clear deliverable with a concrete deadline, don't wait until you deliver the final product to find out whether the deliverable meets the expectations. Instead, check with your boss early on to make sure that you are going in the right direction. That means actually showing the boss drafts or samples of what you are doing, not just describing it. Say, "This is an example of the product I am building. Does this meet your requirements? What adjustments do I need to make?" You are much better off having that conversation early and often so that by the time the deadline rolls around for the final deliverable, there will be no surprises.

Any opportunities you can seize to help your boss spot-check your work will help you identify and solve any hidden problems. For example, if you manage a database, ask your boss to walk through some records at random with you to spot-check them for quality. If you write reports, ask your boss to look at early drafts or draft sections. If you make phone calls, ask your boss if you can record them and listen to a random sample together so he can help you improve. If you make widgets, ask your boss to look at some half-done widgets with you to see how they are coming along.

Ask your boss to watch you work. If you want to make absolutely sure that you are accomplishing a task the way your boss wants you to do it—especially if you are not responsible for producing a tangible end product—one of the most effective ways to get that clarity is to get the manager to watch you work. Watching you complete a task will give her a clear view of what you are doing and how you are doing it. For example, if you are in a customer service role, having your boss watch you interact with a customer will tell her more about your customer service performance than any batch of customer feedback surveys. In particular, if you are having difficulty succeeding with a specific task, ask your boss to "shadow" you while you accomplish the task. If your boss is really good at the task, she is likely to have some good advice for doing it better.

Give your boss an account of your performance. In every one-on-one conversation with every boss, you should be providing a full and honest account of exactly what you've done on your assignments for that boss since your last conversation: "These are the concrete actions I've taken. This is what I did and how I did it. These are the steps I followed in order to meet or exceed the expectations we set together." Once you've given a full and honest account, you and your boss will be better able to clarify next steps. As long as you are engaged in an ongoing, consistent one-on-one dialogue with that boss, this element of helping your boss monitor your performance will become routine.

Use self-monitoring tools. Help your boss keep track of your concrete actions by making good, rigorous use of self-monitoring tools like project plans, checklists, and activity logs. Monitor in writing whether you are meeting the goals and deadlines laid out in a project plan. Make notes and use checklists, and report to your boss at regular intervals. Use an activity log, a diary noting contemporaneously exactly what you are doing all day, including breaks and interruptions. Each time you move on to a new activity, note the time and the new activity you are turning to.

Spread the word. Ask customers, vendors, coworkers, and everyone else you work with to give you honest feedback about your performance in relation to them. Ask them, in writing, "How am I doing?" Consider passing their responses on to your boss. Remember, one of the most consistent sources of information most bosses have about the work of their employees is hearsay. People talk. Word spreads. You should know what people think about your work and use that data as feedback to help you improve. But this feedback will also be important to pass on to your boss so that you have some input in the general hearsay about your work.

WHAT GETS MEASURED AND WHAT SHOULD GET MEASURED?

If you've been in the workplace for any significant length of time, chances are that you have experienced the "annual review" and maybe "the midyear review." Although these types of reviews are standard in many workplaces, many people, managers and employees alike, find them to be, at best, inadequate and incomplete measures of an employee's performance. In the worst cases, many people find formal reviews to be unfair, or even downright capricious. That's because reviews usually fail to truly describe and evaluate the specifics of the employee's day-to-day concrete actions over the course of time.

The only way that periodic reviews can reasonably describe and evaluate performance is when the manager conducts an ongoing and explicit evaluation of an employee's tangible actions measured against clearly stated expectations. Typically, however, when the time comes to write reviews and grade or rank employees, most managers simply scramble to complete the reviews in time, basing evaluations and rankings on the scant records they have kept during the year.

In order to make sure your performance is accurately and fairly measured, you need to help each boss track your actions every day and weigh them against the clear expectations that have been set in advance with that boss. On a continuous basis you need to be asking and answering, in conversation with your boss, the following questions:

- Did you meet every goal that was set? Did you do all the tasks that were required of you? Did you go the extra mile?
- Did you complete the tasks according to the guidelines and specifications provided? Did you follow standard operating procedures? Did you go above and beyond the quality standards?
- Did you meet the deadlines that were set in advance? Did you get the work done even faster?

If you have been helping your boss monitor, measure, and document your concrete actions on a regular basis, answering these questions should simply require a cumulative summary of your regular tracking. This is the most important set of data your boss can ever have about your actual performance. Of course, your boss also has a huge amount of data in the form of daily, weekly, quarterly, or annual reports that detail all sorts of performance information, from attendance and hours worked to customer complaints, sales data, and on and on. So although your boss will use this information too, the key is to help him understand what all those numbers really say about your actual performance—how they are tied (or not tied) to the substantive actions that have been within your control.

Sales numbers, for example, would seem at first glance to be a clear reflection of sales performance. But that is not always the case. Imagine that you are trying to sell a product that has no market reputation, and worse, you are working from a list of unqualified customers, people who are not likely to be buyers of the product. Meanwhile, your colleague is selling a product with a great market reputation, and she is working from a list of qualified buyers. Your colleague's numbers are likely to be significantly better than yours, but for reasons that are actually beyond your control. Thus, the sales numbers alone would not give your boss enough information to adequately measure your performance, especially when comparing your performance to that of your colleague.

How could you help your boss better evaluate your performance? You could ask your boss to look at the number of calls you attempted each day; those at least are actions that are under your control. But to measure your work accurately, the boss would also need to evaluate how you handled each call. Did you listen carefully to the prospective buyer, without interrupting? Did you stick to your sales script? Did you respond well to questions? Did you employ techniques to move the sales conversation to a close? Those kinds of subjective questions would probably matter most when measuring your performance in this situation. It would be up to you to do the hard work of helping your boss evaluate your performance on these actions.

DOCUMENT YOUR PERFORMANCE

Most managers rarely document performance unless they are required to do so. In fact, other than the inadvertent paper trail of automatically recorded data, notes, paperwork, end-product reviews, and e-mail correspondence, there is a good chance that most of your day-to-day work is not documented by anyone. The bulk of your formal personnel file probably consists of mid-year and annual reviews, maybe some annually updated development plans, your rankings (if the company ranks employees), your numbers (when they are tracked), occasional nominations for bonuses and awards—and of course any formal write-ups of misconduct or persistent failure.

Still, in the regular course of business, managers do accumulate random documentation. Take e-mail, for example. Whether you or your boss(es) realize it, e-mail messages may document the details of much of your day-to-day performance. When you use e-mail, especially in dialogue with your boss, you create detailed, contemporaneous records that may often spell out expectations, evaluate work in progress, and record praise for your work, or criticism. Be aware of this, and keep your own "virtual" paper trail of saved e-mails organized in folders.

When do managers most rigorously document performance? Unfortunately, it's often not until an employee has demonstrated serious performance problems for some length of time. In such situations, human resources (HR) provides managers with a formal process for documenting the employee's problematic performance or behavior. This formal documentation process is intended to help the manager meet the requirements for taking disciplinary action. The process usually includes a date and time log for recording verbal requests and verbal warnings, as well as a protocol for written warnings. Usually, after the second or third written warning, the manager can put the employee on what HR professionals call a PIP, which stands for "performance improvement plan."

Here's how the typical PIP works. The manager and the employee meet to spell out in minute detail vividly clear expectations and to work out a plan for what the employee needs to do to improve performance. Goals are broken down into concrete steps and to-do lists with tight deadlines; guidelines and parameters are stated in no uncertain terms. Every week, or sometimes every day, the manager sits down with the employee to evaluate precisely how well the employee's performance has met the expectations set forth in the PIP. In other words, this process actually forces the employee and the manager to engage in the kind of performance-tracking they should have been doing together every step of the way, before any problem with performance existed!

Instead of waiting for a performance problem to rear its ugly head, put *yourself* on a PIP. Call it something else if you like. How about a "Continuous Improvement Plan"? Whatever you call it, this is the perfect format for helping your boss document your performance every step of the way. Together with your boss, spell out expectations for your performance in terms of verifiable actions that you can control. Keep track in writing as you complete each to-do item and meet each requirement; as you achieve each goal and beat each deadline. Regularly report to your boss on exactly how and when your concrete actions met or exceeded the expectations you set together. Help your boss document these facts every step of the way.

CREATE A SIMPLE PROCESS YOU CAN STICK WITH

You need to work out a tracking system for documenting your work for every single boss. But the last thing you or your boss want or need is a lot of cumbersome paperwork that slows everything down. Work out a system that is simple, practical, and easy to use so that you and your boss can stick with it.

One approach is to keep a notebook or a diary in which you take notes all day long about assignments received, goals set, guidelines laid out, intermediate and final deadlines, to-do lists, and concrete actions you take. Include tools such as checklists to guide you in the performance of your work. If you have multiple bosses, consider creating a template for each boss. If you have recurring tasks and responsibilities, consider creating templates for that work. Keep refining your system to streamline it and to make it easier for you to keep track of things in writing.

If you prefer to keep track using electronic tools, all you need is a database and a scheduling program that allow you to create a data record for each boss and each separate work matter. As soon as you receive a new assignment or a change to an existing assignment, enter the information into the electronic record. Create templates for each of your bosses, and for ongoing tasks, responsibilities, and projects. Use the electronic tools to create an ongoing record of your work.

The advantage of electronic tools is that they usually force some logic and organization into your documentation system.

Also, your notes are captured digitally and are automatically dated and time-stamped. You can also cut and paste key e-mail correspondence, including the back-and-forth messages between you and your boss that help document your performance, keeping such text in the notes section of the appropriate record in your tracking system.

Whether you use a notebook or an electronic tool, you should capture certain key pieces of information:

- *Expectations*. Goals and requirements that were spelled out. Instructions given or to-do lists assigned. Standard operating procedures, rules, or guidelines reviewed. Deadlines set and timelines established.

- *Concrete actions*. Your actual work as you complete each to-do item, achieve each goal, fulfill each requirement, and meet each deadline.

- *Measurements*. How your concrete actions are matching up against the expectations. Have you met or exceeded requirements? Did you follow instructions, standard operating procedures, and rules? Did you meet the goals on time?

When you are keeping track, remember that you are creating a contemporaneous record of *your* work performance. Never write down anything personal about a boss, a coworker, a customer, a vendor, or anyone else. Focus on keeping notes about your work, and your work alone. Use specific, descriptive language such as, "Followed Interviewing Guidelines to interview three job applicants," or "Submitted final report for XYZ project three days before the deadline." Don't use vague language or broad words like "slow," "successful," "good," "sloppy," "incomplete," or "difficult." Stick to clear descriptions of your actions in terms of goals, guidelines, and deadlines.

WHEN SHOULD YOU DOCUMENT YOUR PERFORMANCE?

During your one-on-one meetings with the boss, take notes as necessary. Then make notes immediately after the conversation. Between the one-on-one meetings keep notes about anything of consequence. As you think of things you want to report on or ask about in your next meeting, write them down.

Before each one-on-one meeting, check your notes from the last session and make notes in preparation for this one. What performance did you and your boss go over last time? What ground do you want to cover this time? Which of your concrete actions do you want to describe for the boss? What expectations do you want clarified regarding next steps?

During your conversations with your boss, use your written documentation as a visual aid and point of reference. By showing the boss exactly what you are writing down, you will clarify expectations for your performance. This gives both you and the boss a chance to reinforce your understanding of the details and guidelines of the assignment, and an opportunity to correct any misunderstandings up front. As you take notes, you can check with each other: "I'm writing this down. What are you writing down? Are we on the same page?"

When should you document your performance? Here's the simple answer: every step of the way.

CHAPTER EIGHT

Earn More Rewards by Doing More Work, Faster and Better

It's the end of the calendar year. You wonder how your annual review is going to turn out. What ranking will your boss assign you? What rewards will be attached to your ranking? If your boss is like most, I'll bet that she is struggling to complete those annual reviews, to assign those rankings, and allocate those discretionary rewards—if there are any rewards within her discretion.

When it comes to how employees are rewarded, every company is different. That can make it hard for you to figure out how to earn more rewards for your hard work. What if managers in your company are required to rank employees on a bell curve? Will you be one of the select employees who receive a higher ranking and a bigger raise and bonus? If you feel you are a high-performer and you get a middle or lower ranking, you might feel some resentment about this kind of forced ranking of employees and the corresponding compensation system.

On the other hand, what if you work in a company that does not differentiate between and among employees on the basis of performance, where high-performers and low-performers are recognized and rewarded equally? What kind of resentment can this kind of "equality" cause? Who can complain about a system where everyone is rewarded equally? If you've made it this far through the book, there is a pretty good chance that you are a high-performer, and you might be answering, "High-performers, that's who!" And you would have a point.

The truth that everybody knows but nobody likes to acknowledge is that one high-performing employee is worth more to the business than three or four mediocre employees. If you are one of those high-performing employees, you already know that. If you are not one of those high-performing employees, you should learn that truth and become one! And if you want to earn more rewards, it helps to understand how your company makes decisions about when, how, and how much to reward its employees.

CURRENT TRENDS IN PERFORMANCE MANAGEMENT

There are three leading trends lately in human-capital management that affect the way in which employees tend to be rewarded: (1) the new version of "management by objective"; (2) forced ranking; and (3) pay for performance. All three can present obstacles to your attempts to earn more rewards from your hard work.

The new version of "management by objective." These days, managers at all levels are given performance objectives (referred to as "numbers" because they are usually articulated in numbers) for every dimension of their operations. The worthy intention is to place the focus on concrete, measurable out-comes. The problem is that too often the numbers serve as a trigger for cascading recrimination (or praise), even though what gets measured may not be tied directly to actions that are in the control of the employee. Without step-by-step instructions communicated clearly at every level of the chain of command, these objectives can be little more than wishes.

Forced ranking. Most leading organizations are moving to some form of "forced ranking" mentioned at the beginning of this chapter; it is a practice made famous by Jack Welch, the CEO of GE for some twenty years. In this practice managers are required to make candid evaluations of every employee according to a tight distribution of grades such as A, B, and C. While evaluation and differentiation are key in this system, forced ranking is, sadly, an exercise in guesswork unless managers monitor, measure, and document every employee's performance on an ongoing basis. Once a year just won't do the trick.

Pay for performance. This is currently the biggest trend in compensation: decreasing the amount of employee pay that is fixed, and increasing the amount that is contingent on performance. I applaud the notion of differential rewards based on differential performance. The fact is, though, that pay for performance works only when managers spell out for each employee exactly what the person needs to do (concrete actions within the control of the employee) to get paid more, as well as what he or she might fail to do that would result in a decrease in pay. The manager then needs to monitor, measure, and document each employee's actual performance (those concrete actions) on an ongoing basis. But as this often doesn't happen, the results of pay for performance can be surprising and unfair—despite the obvious fairness of the idea.

These three trends are central to the new high-pressure workplace in which high performance is the only option. The irony is that even though each of these strategies is intended to make up for the fact that managers don't engage in more day-to-day performance management with employees, they each depend on a high level of engagement, and they fail miserably when managers are disengaged.

The above trends have several important implications for what you need to do in order to earn more rewards:

- *Make sure you know exactly where you fit in relation to your managers' numbers.* What role do you play? How does your work move the numbers? Talk with each boss to make sure your understanding is right.

- *But don't focus on the numbers.* Instead, focus on your performance of your work in your role.

- *Keep close track of your actions in writing.* Keep track of your concrete actions at work: this is the performance you actually control, and your efforts to meet your goals and deadlines. Keep score for yourself on your contributions so you will be able to describe them to each boss.

- *Make sure you know whether you will be ranked and, if so, when, how, and by whom.* If your company uses a forced ranking system, how does it work? Exactly which aspects of your work will each boss consider when ranking you? Talk with each boss to make sure your understanding is right.

- *Maintain an ongoing dialogue with each boss.* Every step of the way, engage in ongoing conversation to make sure you understand the boss's performance expectations of you for the year, the month, the week, and for today.

Exactly which tasks, responsibilities, and projects should you focus on right now? Exactly which goals and deadlines should you focus on right now? Exactly which to-do items take priority? What are the opportunities to meet requirements, and what are the opportunities to go the extra mile?

- *Try to get each boss involved in ongoing written tracking.* Try to get each boss to document, in writing, how well your actual performance is lining up with the expectations you set together every step of the way. And whether a particular boss keeps track in writing or not, *you* do so as you accomplish each concrete action and every task, responsibility, or to-do item. Keep score for yourself, and show each boss your written tallies during your ongoing one-on-ones about your work.

- *Find out whether you will be subject to a pay-for-performance system.* If so, make sure you understand how the system works. Is there a formula? Who decides? When? How? How much money is at stake? What can you do to earn more? What would result in your earning less? Again, discuss the system with each of your bosses to make sure your understanding is right.

THE DULL BLUDGEON OF TREATING EVERYBODY THE SAME

The sad fact is that in the real world of undermanagement, most managers gravitate to "sameness" because it's easier. Whether it's hourly pay or a fixed salary, if you are paid according to a set system, your boss doesn't have to make and justify difficult decisions about the value of your work. Of course, some "sameness" in rewards is useful. Gym memberships, child care, and other shared rewards benefit all employees. They also add to a feeling of connection to the company, and they contribute to employees' well-being, which probably results in employees who provide a greater return on investment to the company over time.

Beyond the shared rewards, most managers have at least some discretion to differentiate, recognize, and reward employees for exceptional performance—usually more discretion than they actually use. Yet even though a manager might have a discretionary bonus pool and a lot of input on raises, somehow everybody on the team ends up sharing equally in the bonuses and getting roughly the same raises. The same goes for working conditions and special accommodations. Most managers also have a great deal of discretion in work schedules, assignments, working conditions, the allocation of supplies, and so on. Yet many managers simply cannot or will not dedicate the time and energy to make tough performance-based distinctions and then follow through to reward people on what they deserve.

REAL FAIRNESS

I have never met a high-performer who thinks it is fair to give high-performers and low-performers the same rewards. Low-performers love to be treated the same as high-performers. But it's never true the other way around.

The question is, what can *you* do to help your boss(es) help you earn the special recognition and rewards you want and need?

Every boss worth her salt wants to get more work, and better work, out of every employee. As an employee you are doing your best to succeed, and trying desperately to earn what you need and want. If you do more work and better work, then you deserve more. That's only fair.

Of course, no boss can do everything for everybody. But you need to know what performance will be required of you if you are to earn any special recognition or rewards. You need to help your boss define expectations and then tie any concrete rewards directly to the fulfillment of those expectations. That means engaging in an ongoing dialogue with every boss who has any influence or authority over your working conditions and rewards. This includes asking each boss some direct questions:

"Tell me what you need from me every step of the way. What can I do to exceed expectations, to go the extra mile, to step up, to stand out, and to be more valuable to you? Do you want me to arrive early? Stay late? Do you see how I am focused and working hard every minute I'm here? What deadlines do you want me to beat? How can I take exactly the right amount of initiative without overstepping my bounds? Tell me what you need, because there are a lot of things I need and want here, too, and I want to earn those things with my performance. I want to earn them by getting tons of work done very well, very fast, all day long."

YOUR REPUTATION IS THE
SECRET TO MORE LEVERAGE

" 'How do you get the incredible custom deal you have at work?' People ask me that question all the time." That's how Hank, a very self-satisfied research scientist in a major pharmaceutical company, framed our conversation. He continued: "I come and go whenever I please. I make my own schedule. I work from home some days. I work only with the technicians I know and trust. I have the best assignments. My boss lets me go to conferences and training on the company's dime. And I make more money than most of the other professional staff. . . . Plus, I've only been here for four years."

How does Hank get such an incredible custom deal at work? What is his secret for getting such flexible work conditions and such generous rewards?

"It's leverage," Hank explains. "I have real leverage with my boss because I have a reputation for getting things done and getting them done well, ahead of schedule. I'm here early, and I work evenings and weekends if I have to. I'm very careful with resources, so I'm always under budget." Hank continued: "My boss knows he can count on me, and that gives him leverage with his boss when he wants to go to bat for me. He can say, 'I think we should give Hank what he wants because he is doing great work and is going to continue doing great work.' Even if they can't give me something I want, I'm building up a positive balance in my favor in the bank account. Sometimes you have to be patient. It pays off eventually. Eventually they will want to do something more for me because I've built up a reputation for being valuable. They want to keep me happy."

Learn Hank's lesson: Be valuable! If you want to have real leverage with your boss, you have to make your boss want to keep you happy. Build a reputation for doing great work every day by *doing* great work every day. If you are patient and let your value accrue, it will pay off eventually.

Here is Kate's corollary to Hank's lesson. An electrical engineer in a large aeronautics company, Kate was assigned with a small work group to solve an engineering design problem at a remote manufacturing center. When they got to the location, the design team realized that there were obvious flaws through-out the manufacturing process. Two engineers would need to relocate to the remote site for at least a year and work double-time for the foreseeable future.

Says Kate, "I just blurted out, 'I'll do it,' and it was done. Nobody wanted to fight for that job." Why did she volunteer? "It was just naked ambition," Kate explains. "I could sacrifice a year, do nothing but eat, drink, breathe, dream the work. By the end of it, I would have earned a bunch of money. But it was more than that. I knew it would be an incredible learning and growth experience. I would be working with Mandy, the senior engineer who was the team lead, a real rising star on the engineering side, a really good mentor figure for me. I was going to be right in there getting my hands dirty in a working manufacturing process. Here I was at this really key point in my career, working with Mandy on this really exciting work. It was an incredibly grueling experience. I felt like I had been through a medical residency or something. But it was so worth it. The rewards were truly exceptional."

Like Hank, you can get more leverage and earn more re-wards by getting a reputation for doing great work. Like Kate, you can earn truly exceptional rewards by being willing to sacrifice, suffer, and "do nothing but eat, drink, breathe, and dream the work."

Imagine if you could stop getting paid by some fixed sys-tem, locked in the prison of one-size-fits-all sameness. What do you think would happen if you could negotiate with your boss and trade your time, effort, and ideas—your hard work—for some package of rewards?

Here's the funny thing: it is an imperfect system. Most people are not paid in ways that are directly tied to their per-formance. Still, over time, the Rule of Hank will kick in. Your actual performance will be the key to your reputation, your perceived "value," your leverage, and ultimately your ability to earn flexible work conditions and generous rewards. And if you want to jump-start the process, remember Kate's Corollary.

YOU HAVE TO START SOMEWHERE

Of course, not everyone can be a Hank or a Kate, at least not right away. But if like Hank and Kate you want to get into a better position to earn more generous rewards, where do you begin? Start with these two steps:

Step One. Make sure that in your working relationship with each boss, you understand not only how to meet the basic expectations of the job but how to go above and beyond those expectations—and what rewards might be available if you do.

Step Two. Through open communication and transparency, build a working relationship of trust and confidence with the boss. Help your boss monitor, measure, and document your performance every step of the way. If you make a commitment, deliver on that commitment. If you fail to meet a commitment, be honest and forthright about it. Put your boss in a position to let you know whether your work is hitting the target on an ongoing basis.

Don't be a big baby when it comes to acknowledging the fact that you may not have achieved the necessary goal to earn a particular reward. Likewise, don't be too greedy when you do achieve the goal and it's time to collect on promised rewards. If your boss can't deliver on a reward right away, or if a promised reward somehow evaporates, try to be understanding. Write off the loss as a cost of doing business, an investment in the bank account of your working relationship. At least you won't have to wonder whether your performance has been noted and appreciated. Use the appreciation to gather momentum.

By the way, if your boss can't reward you right away but seems to appreciate what you've done, consider asking him to write a letter describing your success, then to give you a copy, place a copy in your employee file, and maybe pass a copy up the line to his boss. This is a good way to help your boss make you feel rewarded rather than jilted in the event a hoped-for reward falls through.

Keep in mind that your boss may not realize how much power she has to influence your rewards. Like so many other managers, yours might have discretionary resources available for rewards but just doesn't use them. She might have some power to influence senior management regarding your rewards but just doesn't wield it. She might be able to jump through hoops to get you more rewards but just doesn't do it. That doesn't mean you should be pressuring her for more rewards all the time. Rather, it means making it obvious to the boss that you *deserve* more rewards, and doing everything you can to help her give you more of the discretionary rewards at her disposal.

Discretionary rewards might include the following:

- *Money and benefits*. How much of your base pay is fixed? How much is contingent on clear performance benchmarks tied directly to concrete actions you can control? What is the value of your benefits? What are the levers you can pull to drive your own compensation up?
- *Work schedule*. What is the default work schedule? How much flexibility is there? What levers can you pull to earn more scheduling flexibility?

- *Relationships.* Who will you be working with? Which vendors, customers, coworkers, subordinates, and managers? What levers can you pull to have more control over whom you get to work with (or not work with)?
- *Tasks.* Which regular tasks and responsibilities will you be assigned to do? Are there any special projects? What levers can you pull to get more opportunities to work on choice tasks, responsibilities, or projects?
- *Learning opportunities.* Will there be any special learning opportunities? What levers can you pull to access more of them?
- *Location.* Where will you be located? How much control will you have over your workspace? Will there be much travel? Are there opportunities to be transferred to other locations? What levers can you pull to control your location?

If you want a custom deal that includes some or all of these key elements of your job, you will need to know what discretionary resources your boss has at his disposal and then help him help you get more of them. What hard work can you offer? What extra effort can you make? What value can you add? What leverage do you have? What can you bring to the table as a bargaining chip to earn more of those discretionary resources? Make sure that the boss feels he is getting a very good bargain—that he will be delighted to make a special arrangement to reward you because you are delivering so much value in return.

So I always tell people to look out for really tough assignments, special projects and roles that are hard to fill. Look for ways you can sacrifice to save your boss trouble. Don't be annoyed when all the pressure is on you—be grateful. This is your big chance to prove yourself and make a huge investment in your career; to build up your professional reputation and a significant positive balance in your management relationship account.

BE REALISTIC

You need to figure out how to "do business" with each boss. You have a right to expect to be recognized and compensated for the work you do. But you don't want any false hope or false promises. If your boss thinks that what you need and want from the job is unrealistic, you will want to know that immediately so that you can adjust your expectations.

"If you want a helicopter . . . that's just not going to happen," said a manager in a nonprofit community service organization. "But if you want free memberships for your family members, that's no problem. If you want to leave early to visit your sick nephew, that's no problem. When employees cooperate with me, I cooperate with them. I can't do everything for everybody all the time. But I will do what I can for you, especially if you are going out of your way to help me out when I need you." Small, one-time accommodations are among the resources that managers do have available to them. "If you want to be on the receiving end of those accommodations, you have to do your part to put me in a position to help you."

Maybe your boss lets you come in a little late or make personal calls from the office because you are otherwise valuable and there are not a lot of discretionary rewards available. If you think that your boss intends those accommodations as a small reward, mention them. Ask whether you have interpreted the situation correctly. Say thank you. Whatever it is, make the quid pro quo explicit. Reassure the boss that you know this custom deal is not to be taken for granted and remains contingent on your continuing to deliver on your part of the deal.

EVERYTHING IS NEGOTIABLE, ALMOST

Employment relationships are transactional by nature. If you want special rewards, find out every step of the way exactly what is expected of you and what you can do to go the extra mile and earn those rewards. Will there be bonuses for early delivery or exceptional quality, or penalties for late delivery or work that fails to meet expectations? The ideal bargain clearly defines the deliverables expected and has an explicit deadline for delivery along with specific milestones that need to be reached along the way. Every ounce of compensation—financial and nonfinancial—would be tied either to a specific milestone you control or to the ultimate delivery by the agreed-on deadline. In an ideal world, if you work smarter, faster, and better, then you get paid more money and are given more flexible working conditions.

Does this mean that everything is open to negotiation? Of course not. In fact, if you are in a position to negotiate special rewards and increased flexibility for yourself, the first thing to consider is what is *not* negotiable. What are the basic requirements of the job, the essential performance standards, and acceptable behaviors? What are the basics for which you should expect nothing more than to be treated fairly and paid for your work? Those are the deal breakers. You have to be very clear with yourself: "For coming in to work on time, for not leaving early, and for getting a lot of work done very well all day long without causing any problems, I get paid. And I get to keep working here!" Doing your job well, fast, all day long is what you were hired to do. That's why you get paid a basic wage or salary. That's why you get the basic benefits. That's why you get to come to the office pizza party.

When you deliver on that deal consistently for some period of time, you put yourself in a position to seize opportunities to go above and beyond the deal and thereby earn more. Keep your eyes peeled for those opportunities. When they present themselves, focus on them like a laser beam. With the value you bring to the table, you will be in a position to negotiate for increased rewards and flexibility. And remember, you'll have much more success if you don't try to negotiate for long-term fixed rewards but rather for small rewards that are tied to measurable performance benchmarks within your control.

OFFER A PROPOSAL

One executive put it this way: "You want something from me? When you ask, I want to know: 'What is the benefit of what you are proposing? Is there a benefit to me? To the company? To the group? What will it take to make this happen? What role are you going to play? Who else is going to be involved? How long is this going to take? Where is this going to happen? How are you going to do it?'"

Indeed, if you answer those questions every time you make a request for a reward of any kind, you will, in effect, be preparing a simple proposal. I have seen this technique work wonders for individuals seeking additional resources or rewards or more flexible working conditions. I've seen it work in organizations of all shapes and sizes.

I once learned a very simple rule from a Marine Corps leader: "Don't make requests lightly, and they won't be taken lightly. Requests are serious business."

Requests *are* serious business. Learn to write a simple proposal if you want more resources for your work; greater financial rewards for yourself or your subordinates; greater access to perks; credit for results achieved; more challenging tasks, responsibilities, or projects; special assignments; training opportunities; exposure to decision-makers; the chance to work in a choice location; scheduling flexibility; or even quirky personal accommodations. If you impose this discipline on yourself, you will tend to make fewer requests. You will also make more reasonable requests and, almost certainly, make requests in a more professional manner.

The very act of putting your requests into a proposal format will cause you to consider those requests more carefully. And the more carefully you consider your requests—the more you are able to show your boss the benefits of what you are proposing to do—the more likely it is that you will be able to earn more, and better, rewards.

CHAPTER NINE

What If Your Boss Really Is a Jerk?

You are feeling frustrated and upset. Your boss is worried, agitated, and getting increasingly angry. You don't want to make things worse—and you certainly don't want to get fired. But it's getting harder and harder not to say something to someone because the boss is being a complete jerk!

Have you ever had a boss who really was a complete jerk? Jerk bosses come in all types: the boss who is intimidating, mean, or abusive; the boss who pretends things are up to you when they are not; the boss who doesn't keep track of what's going on but who makes big decisions that affect everyone; the boss who soft-pedals her authority until something goes terribly wrong, and then comes in and chews you out; the boss who lets small problems slide but comes down like a ton of bricks when a small problem gets out of control; the boss who imposes his obsessions on you; and the boss who wants you to be a beck-and-call-assistant.

Do any of these bosses sounds familiar? Some are worse than others, of course. But if you want to succeed—and keep your sanity—you need to know how to deal with them. And you need to start with yourself.

IS IT THE BOSS, OR IS IT YOU?

Some bosses *are* jerks. But if you think that the description applies to one of your bosses, the first question you should ask yourself is this: Is it really the boss, or is it *me*? Have I been allowing myself to be undermanaged by this boss, or have I been engaging in a regular one-on-one dialogue about my work? Have I been working with the boss to make sure that her expectations for my performance are spelled out clearly, every step of the way? Have I been helping her monitor, measure, and document my performance on an ongoing basis?

Your answers to these questions just might tell you the reasons you have not been getting the guidance, direction, feedback, and recognition you need to succeed in this relationship. Without daily or weekly management conversations, you and this boss have no natural venue in which to discuss how your work is going. You probably talk with this boss only when something is going wrong, and the two of you realize that you absolutely must talk about the work. No wonder the relationship is not going well!

Before you give up on this boss, take a giant step back. Try to manage this boss into a successful working relationship. Figure out what she really needs and wants from you. Start engaging in regular one-on-ones, and help her spell out expectations for your performance. Then monitor, measure, and document your own performance in relation to those expectations. Once you do all that on a consistent basis—customizing your approach to whatever works for this boss—it should be easy to tell whether the problem is you or whether the boss really is a jerk.

IF THE BOSS REALLY IS A JERK

If after you've done the hard work of boss-managing, you are convinced that your boss really is a jerk, you might need to start preparing to jump ship. But what if you are not in a position to take that drastic step, or you need to stall for time in order to get yourself into such a position? What if the upside of the job is so great that you want to find a way to mitigate your boss's jerkiness so that you don't have to quit? Is there anything you can do?

Here's an "outer limits" perspective from an executive who has many years of experience in the television industry: "You can't make it too far in our business unless you know how to deal with jerks. I'm talking about colossal jerks, jerks of every variety. I'm talking about guys who will throw a mug full of coffee at you and then throw the mug.

"The first mistake most people make is losing their cool," says the wise TV executive. "That's rule one when it comes to dealing with the jerk boss: Don't lose your cool. Sometimes you have to remove yourself from the situation so you can calm down and cool off and give the boss a chance to feel bad about being such a jerk. The real rookie move is to get sucked into the dysfunction and get into a pissing match with your boss. You can't win that pissing match."

The executive went on to explain that you have to remain professional, no matter how unprofessional the boss might become. You have to remind yourself that it's not you; it's nothing personal. "Half the battle is staying professional. The other half is to keep talking calmly about the actual work. It's a big mistake to let the boss's bad behavior distract you from the work, because you will still be expected to do it. So keep asking for clear instructions—and then go about your business.

"Most jerk bosses don't act like jerks every minute of every day," he continued. "What you have to do is know when the boss is likely to be in the best possible mood. Maybe you catch the boss the very next morning and then, notes in hand, go in and ask him if you can clarify some things from your discussion the day before: 'Did you mean to say this, that, or the other thing? Did you really want me to tell so-and-so to "F— off and die"?' But never act sarcastic. Never act like you can distinguish between when the boss means something and when the boss doesn't mean something. Treat everything the boss says as if it is serious, write it down, and come back and ask about it the next day. The best-case scenario is that the boss will be reflective and remorseful. He might even apologize and want to talk through what happened.

"The key is to not let the boss off the hook easily. You can say, 'I knew you weren't at your best. I knew you were upset.' Stay professional. Be clear about what happened, get the boss to acknowledge it, and then ask for clear instructions on how to handle it the next time it might happen. . . . And take notes. The key is trying to gain some control over the situation and make it better through your own very professional, rational, and orderly way of doing business."

This approach is echoed by many experienced, successful professionals in other workplaces that are infamous for tolerating jerk bosses. One megastar in the world of investment banking put it this way: "No matter how unprofessional the jerk might be, your best bet is to never blink, never raise your voice, never emit a clue that you are troubled by the boss's behavior. Just read between the yelling, get your marching orders, and go about your business." Why put up with a jerk boss? "You have to do the math for yourself," says the investment banking mega-star. "Can you afford to walk away? Or is there so much upside for you in keeping this job that you can't afford to walk away?

"Actually," she explained, "it is much easier to handle the really egregious cases. The anger-management cases are one thing. . . . It's the more subtle jerks that are sometimes harder to figure out." On the basis of our research I'd have to agree. When a boss is yelling and screaming, it's obvious which one of you is the jerk. But sometimes when a boss is behaving like a jerk—her words and actions related to your work are irrational and disorderly, but they are not overtly abusive—it makes *you* seem like the jerk. Even when that is the case, you need to take the same basic approach. Impose as much rationality and or-derliness as you can on every interaction. Remain professional; keep your cool; take the boss seriously; keep asking for clear instructions; and keep writing things down. If necessary, take a break and come back at a better time to debrief. Review the prior conversation; read from your notes; then ask for clarifica-tion of instructions. If it's appropriate, ask for clear instructions for how to deal with the boss when she is acting like a jerk (but never put it that way, of course).

SEVEN SUBTLE TYPES OF JERK BOSS BEHAVIOR

There's no question that the yelling, screaming, abusive jerks are the worst, and that they can be very painful and difficult to deal with. Let's consider seven subtle types of jerk-boss behavior

and how to apply to each type the withering medicine of rationality, orderliness, and professionalism.

As you read the following scenarios, remember that most
bosses don't want to act like jerks. And despite their best intentions, most bosses will slip into one of these common scenarios at least once in a while. The question is, what can you
do to manage your boss so well that you can help him avoid
such behavior as often as possible?

Jerk-Boss Scenario 1

*The boss lets small problems slide but then comes down like a ton of
bricks when one of those small problems gets out of control, causing
real damage and cost.*

This is the single most common jerk-boss scenario. Almost
all bosses slip into this scenario at least once in a while, unless
they are ever vigilant.

The real problem is that you rarely see this one coming until
it is too late. You think, "This has been going on for weeks. . . .
Why didn't you say something sooner, before it became damaging and costly?"

How does this scenario occur? Instead of engaging in regular and consistent problem solving, this boss finds conversations about problems to be difficult, and tends to avoid them.
If small problems are dealt with at all, they are treated lightly
and in passing—which means they are likely to recur.

Sometimes small problems that recur incessantly finally
cause you or your boss to explode in an outburst of frustration
or anger. Or small problems might become part of the fabric
of your work. Still, some small problems will fester and grow.
Over time, they will become large problems. By the time you

and your boss are forced to talk through what is now a large problem, it's usually too late for the conversation to do much good. Now a great deal of time and energy—yours and the boss's—has to be spent cleaning up the mess. During this time, neither you nor your boss is likely to be at your best. After hours of fixing, salvaging, and cleaning up to get things back on track, you both feel behind on your "real" work. You are both likely to feel demoralized. Sometimes it is hard to bounce back after handling a difficult problem and start feeling good again about the job, and about each other. Sometimes your relationship with the boss goes into a downward spiral.

What can you do to help your boss avoid this jerk-boss scenario?

Every step of the way, keep your eyes out for problems of any kind related to your own work and everything that might affect it. Talk through your work in detail with your boss. Ask your boss for clear, honest feedback about every aspect of your performance.

Think of everything you do and every move you make in your work with this boss as part of a process of continuous improvement. Constantly search for small problems to solve and small improvements that can be made. Keep asking, "What is one thing I could have done better? What is one thing I could do better right now? What is one thing I could do better next time?"

Jerk-Boss Scenario 2

The boss imposes his obsessive-compulsive preferences on you even though there is no clear business reason.

This occurs when the boss is focused on appeasing his own anxiety rather than facilitating your successful completion of the work. Sometimes he wants to look over your shoulder every five minutes. Sometimes he wants you to adhere to an unnecessary schedule of deliverables. He may want you to follow unnecessarily narrow specifications or a needlessly prescribed method.

Don't get me wrong: a boss's close scrutiny of your performance is not jerk-boss behavior. Nor is a boss's requirement that you follow a schedule of deliverables or adhere to narrow specifications or a prescribed method. The behavior is that of a jerk boss when the boss imposes idiosyncratic choices, insisting on personal rather than business reasons. The problem is, you will usually have a hard time making that determination.

What can you do to help your boss avoid this jerk-boss scenario?

Every step of the way, work with your boss to spell out the parameters of every task, responsibility, and project you are doing. Sketch out a project plan, a schedule of deliverables, all the specifications, a stepwise plan of action. If standard operating procedures or best practices are in place for any of the work in question, have them at the ready and walk through them with the boss to explain exactly what you are going to do, how you are going to do it, and why. Then plan to report to the boss at regular intervals, weekly, say, to keep him apprised of your progress.

If the boss insists on giving you her idiosyncratic, eccentric schedule, specifications, and methods, make sure you talk them through with him, pointing out any deviations from standard operating procedures and best practices. Get clarification about exactly what you are being instructed to do and how you are being instructed to do it. Take detailed notes. Go back to your desk and turn those instructions into a project plan, a schedule of deliverables, specifications, and a step-by-step plan of action. Make copies for your boss. Plan to report back at regular intervals to keep the boss informed of your progress.

This approach should keep your boss's anxiety at bay and give him increasing trust in you and your work.

Jerk-Boss Scenario 3

Your boss starts treating you like a beck-and-call-assistant.

This is the boss who never gives you your own tasks and responsibilities but rather keeps you around for one tiny errand at a time. Whenever you are within reach of this boss, you begin to feel like a marionette, being pulled this way and pushed that way: "Hand me this, hand me that. Call so-and-so. E-mail such-and-such. Pick up this, deliver that."

What can you do to help your boss avoid this jerk-boss scenario?

Every step of the way, try to get your boss to give you as many different to-do items as possible in each interaction. Your goal is to get from her lists of to-do items and larger, more complex tasks so that you will have longer and longer timeframes in which you can work independently.

This means you need to keep a pad of paper and a pen (or an electronic tool) handy at all times. Every time your boss engages with you in order to give you an assignment, try to keep the conversation going by asking, "OK. I've got that. Then what?" Try to get more responsibility for larger recurring tasks by paying close attention, asking good questions, taking notes, and learning all the steps. That way, when the larger task recurs, you will recognize it in the boss's initial small-step instructions and you can anticipate the boss's need: "You want me to do A, B, C, D, E, and F, right?"

This approach should help your boss give you a little more space in which to do your work smarter, faster, and better—without pulling your strings the whole time.

Jerk-Boss Scenario 4

The boss starts pretending things are up to you when they are not.

Sometimes the boss is afraid to take charge and doesn't want to boss you around. Sometimes he doesn't want to take the time to explain exactly what is up to you and exactly what is not. Sometimes he doesn't know exactly what needs to be done and how it needs to be done.

You can usually sense this scenario unfolding when you hear the boss say, "Take a crack at it. Do it however you think it should be done." Ask yourself, "Hmmm . . . is it really up to me what I do and how I do it?" If the answer is "Probably not," then you had better ask!

What can you do to help your boss avoid this jerk-boss scenario?

Every step of the way, force your boss to spell out every re-quirement and every expectation for every task, responsibility, and project. Ask for rules, regulations, established best practices, and standard operating procedures. Ask whether there are any checklists. Ask for examples and work samples on which you can base your work. If none of these tools are available, then make your own plan, your own to-do list, and your own check-list, all in writing, and run them by the boss before starting the work. Explain, "This is exactly what I'm going to do and exactly how I am going to do it." That way, you can avoid wasting a lot of time and effort doing the wrong work in the wrong way.

Jerk-Boss Scenario 5

The boss isn't keeping track of what's going on, but makes big deci-sions that affect everyone.

Sometimes the boss is uninformed—or misinformed. Some-times the boss has no idea what she doesn't know.

Don't get me wrong: the fact that a boss shows up suddenly and makes a big decision that affects everyone doesn't make the boss a jerk. Nor does the fact that she may be uninformed or misinformed. What makes jerk-boss behavior is when the boss expends little effort to keep track of who is doing what, where, why, when, and how, and then makes big decisions anyway!

What can you do to help your boss avoid this jerk-boss scenario?

Every step of the way, keep your boss informed, and be a very reliable source of honest, accurate, and complete information. Be the boss's eyes and ears on the ground and report to her regularly. Keep her apprised of exactly what you are doing, why you are doing it, and how, where, and when you are doing it. Report any important information you think she should know. But make sure you are not gossiping and tattling on coworkers— talk only about the work. If your boss is uninformed or misinformed, then become a consistent but always purely professional and businesslike source of information—the what, who, where, when, why, and how—about the work that is being done.

Jerk-Boss Scenario 6

The boss soft-pedals his authority until something goes terribly wrong, and then becomes authoritarian when a strong disagreement arises.

Sometimes the boss is uncomfortable with his own authority. This is the boss who says, "Don't refer to me as your 'boss.' We work together. You don't work 'for me.' We are colleagues, partners."

Sometimes this boss builds false rapport based on effacing the authority component of the relationship and pretending to have a friendship. Sometimes the boss wants to feel like one of the gang.

Building a friendly rapport with his direct reports does not make the boss a jerk. Jerk-boss behavior is when the "friendly" boss becomes authoritarian as soon as the situation gets serious.

What can you do to help your boss avoid this jerk-boss scenario?

Every step of the way, acknowledge the boss's authority and power in your working relationship. Help him build authentic rapport with you by talking about the genuine terrain you have in common: the work you do together. Every time your boss tries to shoot the breeze about personal stuff, talk about the work. Ask for guidance, direction, and support. When he says, "Don't refer to me as your boss," remind him that "Gosh, actually you are my boss, and that matters a lot." Talk about your goals and deadlines, your projects and plans; talk about your performance and what you can improve; talk about your training needs and work conditions; talk about your career aspirations. Remind him how much authority and influence he has when it comes to your career, and how much you appreciate his support.

Jerk-Boss Scenario 7

The boss is intimidating, mean, or abusive.

Sometimes a boss yells and screams, threatens, makes insults, or even uses violence. Why?

Some bosses have anger-control issues. Some just revel in being at the top of the heap. It makes them feel important. It's the workplace version of schoolyard bullying. It is also irresponsible and damaging.

What can you do to help your boss avoid this jerk-boss scenario?

First, remember that this is the boss's psychological problem, not yours. Remember the advice from the television executive and the investment banker: Stay professional. Never blink. Never raise your voice. Get your marching orders and go about your business. And keep detailed notes: dates, times, and concrete examples of what the boss did and said.

The real question in this situation (and it's true for all of the jerk-boss scenarios) is this: Has the boss's behavior been so "jerky" that it's obvious to both of you? Is there an episode or a pattern of behavior—a series of episodes—that you and your boss can discuss? If so, try to get your boss to discuss what happened, to acknowledge it, and to give you clear instructions for what you should do if it happens again. Of course, you risk angering your boss. You might even be putting your job on the line. But if you really can't keep working for this boss under these circumstances, you might consider this approach.

If your boss's behavior is an ongoing problem that you really can't handle, and you don't want to—or can't—walk away, you might have to take a big chance. After you have compiled a detailed record of the abuse, you might report the behavior to senior management, HR, the legal department, or the Equal Employment Opportunity Commission. But it's best to avoid this if you can.

PREPARING FOR A TOUGH CONVERSATION WITH AN ABUSIVE BOSS

Once you've determined that there has been a clear episode or a series of episodes of abusive behavior, you need a game plan for staging a purposeful debriefing session with the boss. This will not be an easy conversation, but it could be a very positive one.

First, review your notes from each jerk-boss episode. Make sure you have all the pertinent details: dates and times that the boss has behaved like a jerk, along with detailed descriptions of the boss's words and actions, and the consequences of those words and actions.

Second, consider your role in each episode. Are you confident you've done a thoughtful, thorough job of trying to help your boss avoid the jerk behavior? Have you remained professional every step of the way? Create a script for yourself so you can stay on track during the conversation. Try to anticipate what the boss might say.

During the meeting, clarify that you want to debrief the episode or series of episodes. Then make sure you do the following:

- Present the facts as you've documented them. Be as specific as you can. Use descriptive words, and mention the dates, times, and details of the situation(s).

- Ask the boss whether she agrees with your account. If she does not, ask her to describe the situations as she experienced them.

- Ask for clear instructions about exactly how the boss wants you to handle yourself in the future if a similar situation should occur. Specifically, how should you interact with her if she repeats the same sort of words and actions.

WHEN THE BOSS WON'T STOP ACTING LIKE A JERK

If the jerk boss just won't stop acting like a jerk despite your repeated efforts to build a better working relationship, you might have to try another approach or find a way to extricate yourself from the situation. You could look for another boss in the same organization. You could go over the boss's head or take your case to an independent third party. Or you might need to quit.

Depending on the situation, you might begin by going manager-shopping. Look around for other managers who appreciate you and can help you do your best work. Try to get one of them to scoop you up and keep you so busy that the jerk boss can't get anywhere near you.

Quitting your job is of course the ultimate solution for getting away from a jerk boss. But maybe you can keep your job and get rid of the jerk instead by going over the boss's head or to an independent third party. There are in fact some good reasons to consider taking the problem to your boss's boss or to someone in HR:

- If the boss is a hopeless jerk, the costs to the organization may be much greater than anybody realizes. You owe it to the organization to make sure someone higher up knows about what's going on.

- This boss might be bad-mouthing you all over the organization. You need to let someone know that the relationship didn't fail because of you.

- If you should want any legal recourse in the future, you will be much better off if you have followed your employer's formal grievance process. Step one will be to go to your boss's boss or to HR.

Of course, going over your boss's head or to HR with a complaint is an unpleasant, scary process. My strong advice is, don't do it lightly. Make sure you have done everything within your own power to deal with the situation first, because once you go outside it, you won't be able to come back. You don't want to seem like a litigious employee, a complainer, or a troublemaker. You need to make it obvious that it wasn't you but rather the boss who made all the trouble.

CHAPTER TEN

Start Here

You have almost finished reading *It's Okay to Manage Your Boss*. You are ready—even eager—to start building more highly engaged relationships with each and every boss. You have set up one-on-one meetings with each boss, just like the book says. In fact, you have a meeting this morning, and you are ready, with a notebook under your arm.

Your new approach takes your boss a little by surprise. But she says to herself, "He's been walking around with that book all week. He's obviously trying something new. I wonder if he'll be able to stick with it. Or will this new thing just blow over?"

Should your boss take you seriously? Will this "new thing" blow over or not? The answers are entirely up to you.

Maybe you have become inspired to take responsibility for your role and your conduct in every single management relationship. You are making real changes so that you are managing every boss more closely for a while.

Then reality sets in. You are incredibly busy, and you realize that this new approach can be very time-consuming, especially at first. Perhaps one of your bosses has been complaining that you are asking too many questions, asking for too much guidance and direction, too much feedback. Some of your peers may be thinking you have been too "intense" lately, too focused on your work. Some might even have whispered, "Hey, slow down. You're making me look bad."

Now you start to think that maybe this new approach isn't such a good idea. Maybe you're just not good at it. After all, you've never been the "most valuable player" before. Before long, you find yourself backing away from your new approach, quickly and steadily, until you are back to the status quo.

"Phew! I'm glad that's over," you might think as you go back to the familiar routine of being disengaged from your boss or bosses. Of course, there are difficult interactions when you and a boss have to go back to solving problems that never had to happen in the first place. But at least, when those hassles are over, you and everyone else can go back to being disengaged until the next unnecessary crisis erupts. You can all go back to pretending that everything is going just fine.

THE DECISION TO CHANGE
IS TOO IMPORTANT TO RUSH

Throughout this book I've tried to convince you to become much more engaged in managing yourself and taking responsibility for your role in every management relationship by actively managing every boss you work with, on any task and for any period of time.

That is my mission: to improve the working relationships between hard-working people and those who lead them. I want you to dedicate yourself to being strong, disciplined, and all about the work. I want you to hold yourself to a higher standard and work more closely with every single boss. I want you to get in there and take responsibility for your part of every management relationship. But, first, you have to take a giant pause and decide whether you are really ready for change.

Think, and think again: Am I ready, willing, and able to commit the time, energy, effort, and consistency that it will take to change? Am I prepared to become a most valuable player for every boss? Am I prepared to be great at managing myself? Am I prepared to be great at managing my relationship with every boss? My role at work is going to change. My relationships at work are going to change. My experience at work is going to change. I am going to be all about the work, setting myself up for success every day, helping my boss help me every day, every step of the way. That's going to be me from now on.

Are you sure you are ready?

CONSIDER THE CULTURE OF YOUR WORKPLACE

Before making a big change in your approach to managing yourself and your boss, you also need to think about the culture of your workplace. Does the culture support strong, ambitious, success-minded people who try to go the extra mile? Or are people in your workplace pretty low-key? Are most of the people in your organization all about the work and highly engaged in an ongoing management conversation with every boss? Or is almost everybody working at an arm's-length distance from their bosses? Are most of the bosses strong and highly engaged, or are they more hands-off? In the context of this corporate culture, what will it mean for you to become someone who is always going the extra mile, who is all about the work, who is engaged in an ongoing management conversation with every boss? Will you fit in? Or will you become something of a maverick?

Here are some of the things that people tell me about the culture in their organizations:

- "This organization is very conservative. We don't believe in confrontation. The culture is very low-key."

- "This organization is very progressive. Everybody sort of does their own thing, and the managers don't like to boss people around. We are pretty low-key and hands-off."

- "Our organization is very large, and there is lots of red tape and bureaucracy, so the culture is for disengaged, low-key, hands-off management relationships."

- "Our organization is very small, and there is more of a family dynamic in the workplace. The culture is for disengaged, low-key, hands-off management relationships."

- "Our work is very technical (or very creative), so the management relationships tend to be disengaged, low-key, and hands-off."

- "Our employees are much older (or younger, or low-level, or high-level), so the culture is disengaged, low-key, and hands-off."

You probably noticed something similar in each of these statements. That's because there is an undermanagement epi-

demic throughout workplaces, at all levels, and in organizations of all shapes and sizes. So, of course, most corporate cul-
tures support management relationships that are disengaged,
low-key, and hands-off.

What can *you* do about it?

Be different. And don't keep it a secret. Stand out as the
ambitious, success-minded person who is all about the work
and who always goes the extra mile. If being serious about your
work and insisting on highly engaged relationships with every
boss makes you a maverick in your organization, then be a maverick. Being different can be uncomfortable. Do it anyway. Be
the person who is not afraid to be strong.

You might find out that the culture supports good management of bosses after all. There may be more highly engaged
management relationships going on than you realize, occurring
just beneath the radar. Or you may find that your example is an
inspiration to others.

Deciding to become highly engaged with every boss is a
big step. If you think you are ready, then it is time to commit
to make a permanent change and to remind yourself of that
decision over and over again.

FOCUS FIRST ON YOUR OWN SELF-MANAGEMENT

The first thing you need to do is to make sure that the first
person you are managing every day is *yourself*. Take good care
of yourself outside of work so that you can bring your best
self to work every day. Arrive a little early to work and stay
a little late. Focus on playing the role assigned to you before
trying to reach beyond that role. Focus on doing your tasks,

responsibilities, and projects very well, very fast, all day long. If you want to carry weight with your boss, that should be your primary focus. Be a problem-solver, not a complainer. Commit to continuous improvement through rigorous self-evaluation.

Think about context and figure out where you fit in every situation. Continually ask yourself, "Where do I fit in this picture? Why am I here? What is at stake for me? What is my appropriate role in relation to the other people in the group? What is my appropriate role in relation to the mission?" Concentrate on playing those roles 110 percent. Contribute your very best thoughts, words, and actions. No matter how lowly or mundane or repetitive or minor your tasks and responsibilities might seem in relation to the overall mission, play your role to the max. Attitude matters—a lot. Effort matters—a lot.

Start mastering the art of human relations. Approach every relationship by focusing on what you have to offer the other person rather than on what you might want or need. Be a model of trust. Remove your ego. Listen carefully. Empathize. Exhibit respect and kindness. Speak up and make yourself understood. Be a motivator. Celebrate the success of others.

Make yourself a great workplace citizen. Under-promise and over-deliver. Don't bad-mouth others, and try not to speak about others unless they are present. Keep your word. Keep confidences. Be an accurate source of information. Don't keep other people waiting. Instead of under-dressing, overdress. Practice old-fashioned good manners.

TALK TO YOUR BOSS(ES)

Once you have self-management under control, it's time to talk to your bosses. Most bosses will be delighted to hear that you want to work harder, that you want to commit to working more closely with them, that you want to take responsibility for your part of the management relationship. Most bosses will be happy to help in your efforts. But if one or more of your bosses is going to be an obstacle, it's important to find that out right away.

When you first talk to a boss, spell out exactly what you are trying to accomplish. Be honest with her. Ask whether she supports your efforts and explain that you need her help and guidance. Talk about coming up with some standard operating procedures to guide the two of you as you work together.

After you talk to each boss, consider other key partners and colleagues you need to apprise of any coming changes. Think about how the changes are likely to affect the people with whom you interact routinely and who interact routinely with your employees. Sit down and talk with all the people you need to prepare or enlist, one by one. Tell them your plan. Ask for their support.

By now you should be pretty warmed up. With any luck, you will be even more committed to change as a result of these conversations.

TAKE IT ONE BOSS AT A TIME, ONE DAY AT A TIME

Never forget that every boss is different. Every boss has his own style, preferences, and habits when it comes to managing. Every boss has his own standards when it comes to evaluating your work. Work out in advance with each boss the details of how you will be held accountable by that boss.

Everything will be a whole lot easier if you establish ground rules up front. In your initial conversations with each boss about how you are going to work together, discuss some of the broader goals, such as productivity, quality standards, and measurable results; how you can make a valuable contribution; and even intangibles like attitude and demeanor.

The most important thing you need to agree on both at the outset of your working relationship and on an ongoing basis is the communication practices you will observe together. How often will you meet, and for how long? What will those meetings cover? Remember, it's best to establish a regular place and time for your one-on-ones. Try to agree in advance roughly how long your meetings will last (my advice is to keep them to fifteen to twenty minutes with a fast and tidy agenda).

Like everything else, this dynamic process will change over time. But the goal is to create a constant feedback loop to clarify expectations, check on resources, measure performance, troubleshoot, make course corrections, and keep your work for that boss moving forward. You want to give every boss an ongoing account of your performance in every one-on-one meeting: Have you met your short-term goals? Have you accomplished everything on your to-do list? Have you met or exceeded the guidelines and specifications? Has your performance been timely and swift? Have your results been of high quality? Have you gone the extra mile? Most importantly, what do you need to do to refine your priorities, work plan, schedule of deliverables, and next steps in your work for that boss?

FINE-TUNE YOUR APPROACH FOR EACH BOSS

When you start having individual meetings with each boss, the differences between your bosses will jump right out at you.

Over time, try to fine-tune your approach to each boss by continually asking yourself these six key questions:

- Who is this boss at work?
- Why do I need to manage this boss?
- What do I need to talk about with this boss?
- How should I communicate with this boss?
- Where should I talk with this boss?
- When should I talk with this boss?

These six questions make up one of the most powerful tools I've ever encountered for tailoring your approach to interacting with different people. I call this tool the "customizing lens." I've used it to help tens of thousands of seminar participants tune in to their managers, their coworkers, and the employees they manage. In fact, you can use this tool to fine-tune your approach to interacting with anyone, inside or outside the workplace.

START MANAGING YOUR BOSSES

The hard part is getting in the habit of making time every day (or every other day, or once a week) to have regular, one-on-one management conversations with every boss you answer to at any given time to discuss the work you are doing with that boss. It will take time to develop the new habit, and time to get used to it—not just for you but also for the bosses you are going to be managing so much more closely.

Take the initiative. Figure out how often you need to meet with each boss, and schedule a regular one-on-one management meeting with each one. Make sure from the outset to keep your management conversations brief, straight, and to the point. Prepare in advance so that you can move the conversation along swiftly.

Focus the ongoing dialogue with every boss on the four management basics:

- Exactly what is expected of you
- The resources you need to meet those expectations
- How you are doing—honest feedback about your performance and what adjustments you need to make
- Credit and reward for your hard work

Over time, you will build an increasingly better working relationship with your boss. As each of you uses your growing knowledge of the other and the overall situation to guide you during each conversation, the stronger and more informed your management conversations will become.

CLARIFY EXPECTATIONS AND TRACK YOUR PERFORMANCE

Remember that the first of the management basics you need from any boss is clear expectations about every aspect of the work you are doing for that boss. Work with each boss at the outset of any assignment to spell out clear expectations; then revisit, revise, and adjust those expectations every step of the way. Make sure you understand exactly what you are expected to do and how you are expected to do it.

The key elements of clarifying expectations are

- Clear goals—a list of concrete deliverables

- Clear guidelines for each goal—a statement of all the specifications and requirements for that goal
- Real deadlines for every goal—a schedule of deliverables with all the steps necessary to meet each deliverable

Early in your transition to highly engaged boss-managing, you need to develop a simple, practical system that will make it easy for both you and your boss to keep track of your performance in writing. No matter what your system, you need to capture the key pieces of information you have learned about in this book: expectations, including goals, requirements, instructions, and deadlines; the concrete actions you take to meet each expectation; and the measurements of how well your actions have met the expectations. Focus on keeping notes on your work, and your work alone. Stick to clear descriptions, and document your performance every step of the way.

START INCLUDING RESOURCE PLANNING

Early in your process, resource planning should be a regular part of your ongoing conversations with every boss on every assignment, task, responsibility, or project you are doing for that boss.

Remember, step one in resource planning involves a daily inventory of primary resource needs. The real key here is planning all the time so that you are always building in enough turnaround time for every resource acquisition. Turnaround time equals the time for processing your request, plus enough time for preparing the resource, plus the time for delivery of the resource to you, plus enough time for you to receive the resource and begin using it. So you are always trying to keep delivery at least one step ahead of your needs.

Step two in resource planning is "supply chain research." *You* need to figure out whether the needed resource is available, what the source is, and what the process, cost, and turnaround time for obtaining that resource might be.

In step three, when resources are unavailable, identify possible workarounds, that is, a plan to complete the job by working around the lack of the resource.

STAY FLEXIBLE: REVISE AND ADJUST

After you have been managing your boss closely for six weeks or so (usually six weeks is enough time to see some big results), the nuances of your challenge will become increasingly clear. You will have gotten over the surprises. You will have done a lot of adjusting. Your one-on-ones will start to feel like standard operating procedure. If you've been monitoring, measuring, and documenting your performance, you will have accumulated a written record that can help your boss fine-tune her approach to managing you that can help you zero in on your own process of continuous improvement.

Keep meeting with your boss regularly. Keep monitoring and measuring and documenting. Continue to revisit your schedule and work plans and to-do lists regularly. Trust the process. Stay flexible. Be prepared to revise and adjust every step of the way as circumstances change.

LEARN TO EARN

After you've been doing the hard work of managing your boss for at least a few weeks, it will be time to start including some discussion of rewards in your ongoing management conversations. Ask regularly what you can do to exceed expectations, to go the extra mile, to step up, stand out, and be more valuable so that you can earn more of the discretionary resources at your boss's disposal. Help your boss tie any concrete rewards you hope to earn directly to the fulfillment of the expectations you have both agreed on.

WHAT ABOUT YOUR COWORKERS?

Once you are in the habit of managing yourself and your boss more closely, you'll need to manage relationships with your coworkers as well. You don't need permission from your coworkers to be strong and maintain highly engaged working relationships with every boss. But you can definitely use your coworkers' support.

Most coworkers will be delighted to hear that you want to work harder and be a more effective member of the team. But a few might present an obstacle to your efforts. Some might feel as if you are making them look bad. Others might resent your efforts because they think you are trying to get some special advantage.

Be honest. Spell out exactly what you are trying to accomplish. Then ask directly whether they support your efforts. Explain that you would like their support and will be happy to support them if they choose to pursue a similar effort. Finally, whether you are committing to mutual support or not, try to at least come to an understanding about how you are going to work together.

If one or more of your coworkers don't believe in highly engaged management relationships, buy them a copy of this book. Try to persuade them to accept and support at least some of what you are trying to do. If you are not able to persuade them, smile and be strong anyway. If your coworkers are disengaged from their boss(es), they will become less and less effective in the workplace, and less and less powerful, while you will become more and more effective, and more and more powerful. The results will speak volumes and might cause your coworkers to reconsider.

GET READY, GET SET . . .

I said at the beginning and I want to remind you again: this book is for people who want to be high-performers. In order to be a high-performer in today's workplace, you need bosses who are strong and highly engaged. If you want your bosses to be strong, you have to help them; you need to be the person who helps weaker bosses get strong, and strong bosses get stronger.

We took everything we learned from fifteen years of interviewing employees and training managers and developed a catalog of dozens of concrete tactics for real-world boss-managing. This book has presented those tactics, organized into a step-by-step approach. We know that the tactics work. If you start practicing them, you will soon be the employee who can say to every boss:

"Great news! I'm going to take responsibility for my part of this management relationship. I'm going to help you manage me. I'm going to work with you every step of the way to make sure I understand in vivid detail exactly what you expect of me on every task, responsibility, and project. I'm going to keep track of my own performance in writing to help you see everything I'm doing and exactly how I'm doing it. I'm going to ask for candid feedback and direction from you, and I want you to give it to me straight. Of course, I want to earn more money and better working conditions and more flexibility. With your help, I'm going to become more and more valuable so it should be much easier for you to reward me!"

It's okay to manage your boss. You just need to get really good at it!

ACKNOWLEDGMENTS

I thank, first and foremost, the thousands upon thousands of people who have shared the lessons of their own experiences in the workplace with me and my company since we began our research in 1993.

Thanks to all those leaders who have given us the chance to work with your organizations over the years. Thanks to the hundreds of thousands who have attended my keynote addresses and seminars. Thanks to the thousands and thousands who have shared so much with me in conversations, interviews, surveys, focus groups, seminar discussions, and e-mails. And thanks to the tens of thousands of managers who have participated in our back-to-basics management seminars. Every one of you is my teacher; without you, I would know nothing. By letting me help you wrestle with your real challenges in the workplace, you have given me real-world lessons every day, which I can bring to others, both through this book and in our seminars.

To those individuals whose stories appear in this book, I offer my infinite thanks. I've tried to give you some anonymity by mixing up some of the less important details.

To my partners at RainmakerThinking, Jeff Coombs and Carolyn Martin, thank you both for your commitment to this enterprise: although Carolyn is retired from our business and is now a full-time poet, we still turn to her for sage advice whenever she is willing. Thank you, Carolyn, for your many contributions to my thinking and writing over the years and for your treasured friendship. Jeff, Jeff, Jeff—each time I write a book, I try to find a new way to thank you. Jeff has long been one of my very best friends. He runs RainmakerThinking, Inc. I trust him with my company, and with my life. I love Jeff like a brother. What else can I say?

Susan Ingraham is much more than an office manager at RainmakerThinking. We have depended on Susan in so many ways since she first came to us around the turn of the millennium. We intend to continue depending on her until—well, I guess, until we all agree to retire. We are truly so deeply grateful for everything you do to make our lives and work so much easier and better. Thank you, Susan, from the bottom of my heart.

To my publishers at Jossey-Bass, thank you for your faith in this book.

Genoveva Llosa has now edited three—count 'em, three—of my books: the present book; *It's Okay to Be the Boss*; and *Not Everyone Gets a Trophy*. She is a total pro: she is smart, easy to work with, and she actually edits. She edits thoroughly and intelligently and makes it seem so much easier than it is. Thank you, Genoveva, for your diligence, kindness, and wisdom. Thanks also to Janis Chan, who had to pinch-hit for Genoveva in the late innings of this book.

Then there is Susan Rabiner, my agent and also Debby's (my wife). Susan is simply the smartest and the best. She and her husband, Al Fortunato, wrote *the* book about writing and publishing nonfiction, *Thinking Like Your Editor: How to Write Great Serious Nonfiction—and Get It Published*. Susan is 100 percent responsible for my success as a writer. How can I thank you enough?

My family and friends are the anchors of meaning in my life. First, thanks to my parents, Henry Tulgan and Norma

Propp Tulgan. I dedicate this book to you both to thank you for raising me as well as you did. You are among my very closest friends to this day, and I treasure the time we spend together.

Thanks to my parents-in-law, Julie and Paul Applegate; my nieces and nephews, being, from oldest to youngest, Elisa, Joseph, Perry, Erin, Frances, and Eli; my sister, Ronna, and my brother, Jim; my sister-in-law, Tanya; and my brothers-in-law, Shan and Tom. I love every one of you very, very much.

I always add a special thanks to my niece Frances because I have always thought of her as my own child. Thanks for everything you are, Frances dear.

Finally, I must always reserve my last and most profound thanks for my wife, Debby Applegate. I always feel so fortunate to have her Pulitzer Prize–winning eyeballs read my manuscript line by line and her fancy pencil making notes throughout the pages. Thank you, dear Debby, for applying some of that world-class talent to making my book so much better. People think I'm exaggerating when I say I remain awestruck by Debby, even after all these years together. Around 1985, Debby started rocking my world on a daily basis. I am fond of saying that Debby is my constant adviser, my toughest critic, my closest collaborator, the love of my life, my best and smartest friend, my partner in all things, half of my soul, owner of my heart, and the person without whom I would cease to be.

ABOUT THE AUTHOR

Bruce Tulgan is an adviser to business leaders all over the world and a sought-after speaker and seminar leader. He is the founder of RainmakerThinking, Inc., a research, consulting, and management-training firm. Bruce is the author of the classic book *Managing Generation X* as well as the recent bestseller *It's Okay to Be the Boss*; *Winning the Talent Wars*; *Not Everyone Gets a Trophy*; and eleven Manager's Pocket Guides. His work has been the subject of thousands of news stories around the world. He has written pieces for numerous publications, including the *New York Times*, *USA Today*, the *Harvard Business Review*, and *Human Resources*. Bruce also holds a fourth-degree black belt in classical Okinawan Uechi Ryu karate. He lives with his wife, Dr. Debby Applegate, winner of the 2007 Pulitzer Prize for Biography for her book *The Most Famous Man in America*. Bruce can be reached by e-mail at brucet@rainmakerthinking.com. His V-log is available weekly for free at www.rainmakerthinking.com.

INDEX